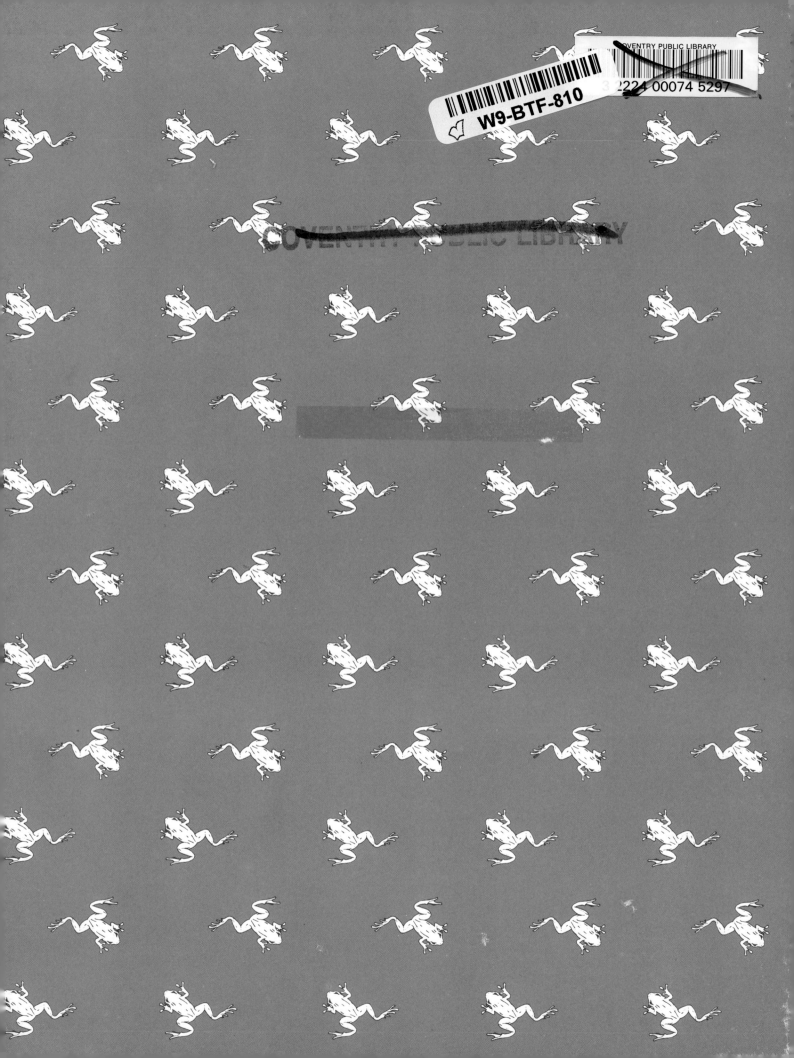

POND
& RIVER

Swan mussel shell

Water snail shell

Common reed

Common reed
fruiting head

Otter skull

Kingfisher skull

Mayfly

Reed-mace
fruit

Mallard egg

Reed bunting nest
and eggs

Great diving beetle

Kingfisher wing

Bittern egg

Snipe egg

Banded demoiselle damselfly

Great ram's-horn shell

EYEWITNESS BOOKS

POND & RIVER

Written by
STEVE PARKER

Wandering snail shells

Trout

Great pond snail shell

Hornwort

Southern hawker dragonfly

Tufted duck skull

Pintail feather

Teasel heads

ALFRED A. KNOPF • NEW YORK

Curly
waterweed

Floating pondweed leaves

River snail

Fern

Yellow flag seeds

Water bird
feather

Water beetle

Bog
pondweed
leaves

Azolla
water
fern

Water
boatman

Water
starwort

Project editor Sophie Mitchell
Art editor Pamela Harrington
Managing art editor Jane Owen
Special photography Philip Dowell
Editorial consultants
The staff of the Natural History Museum, London

Three-spined
sticklebacks

This Eyewitness Book has been
conceived by Dorling Kindersley Limited
and Editions Gallimard

Water bird
feather

This is a Borzoi Book
published by Alfred A. Knopf, Inc.

Dragonfly
larva

Published in the United States by Alfred A Knopf,Inc., New York.
Distributed by Random House, Inc., New York.
Published in Great Britain by Dorling Kindersley Limited, London.
Manufactured in Singapore
0 9 8 7 6
Library of Congress Cataloging in Publication Data
Parker, Steve.
Pond & river/written by Steve Parker; photography by Philip Dowell.
p. cm - (Eyewitness books)
Includes index.
Summary: A photo essay about the range of plants and animals
found in freshwater throughout the year, examining the living
conditions and survival mechanisms of creatures dwelling at the
edge of the water, on its surface, or under the mud.
1. Pond ecology - Juvenile literature. 2. Stream ecology - Juvenile literature.
I. Dowell, Philip. II. Title. III: Title: Pond and river.
QH541.5.P63P37 1988   574.5'26322 - dc19   88-1575
ISBN 0-394-89615-7
ISBN 0-394-99615-1 (lib. bdg.)

Mare's-tail

Water lily leaves

Color reproduction by Colourscan, Singapore
Typeset by Windsor Graphics, Ringwood, Hampshire
Printed in Singapore by Toppan Printing Co. (S) Pte Ltd.

Great pond snails

Hornwort

Contents

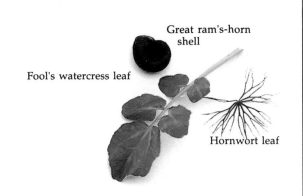

Great ram's-horn shell

Fool's watercress leaf

Hornwort leaf

Spring plants

AFTER THE DULL, COLD DAYS of winter, spring is here at last. There are more hours of sunlight each day, and temperatures are rising. For plants, it is the beginning of the annual race for a place in the sun. In general, the tiny algae, duckweeds, and other small plants are first to show their growth, since each one is small and needs relatively little food. But around the pond, and in marshy areas elsewhere, the irises, reeds, and other colonizers are also showing new green shoots and leaves. All the plants shown below were collected from around a pond on a spring day. They give an idea of the species you may find, although there will always be variations from pond to pond.

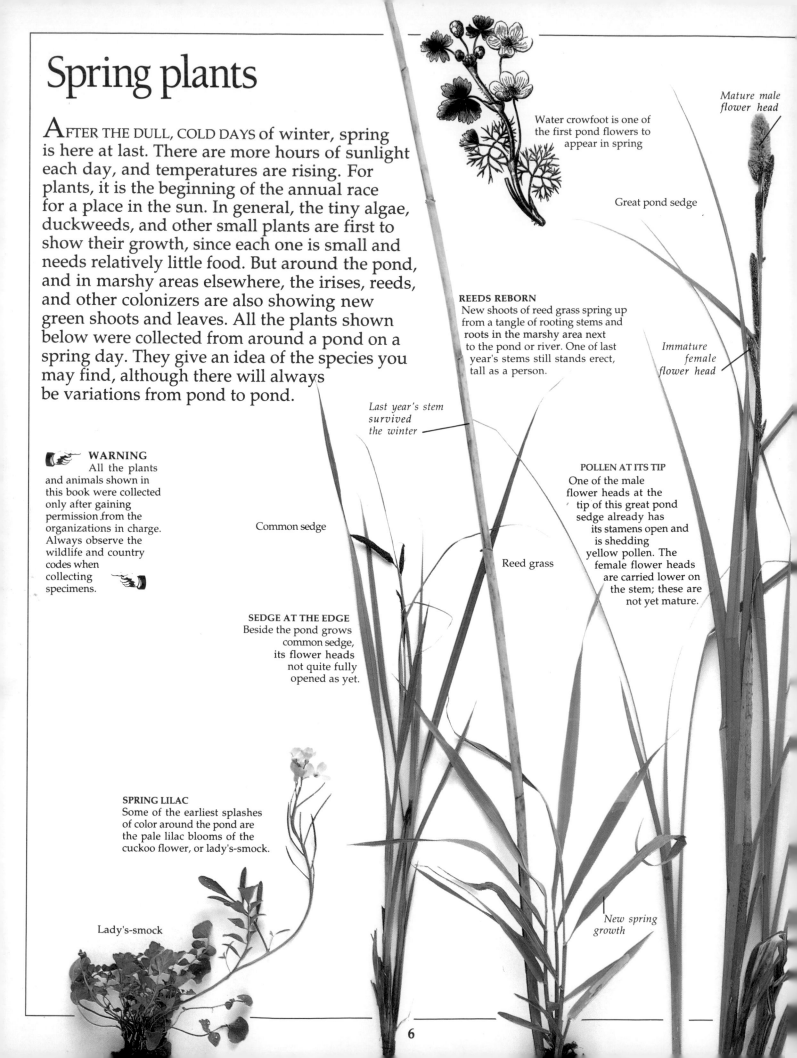

Water crowfoot is one of the first pond flowers to appear in spring

Mature male flower head

Great pond sedge

☞ WARNING
All the plants and animals shown in this book were collected only after gaining permission from the organizations in charge. Always observe the wildlife and country codes when collecting specimens. ☞

REEDS REBORN
New shoots of reed grass spring up from a tangle of rooting stems and roots in the marshy area next to the pond or river. One of last year's stems still stands erect, tall as a person.

Last year's stem survived the winter

Immature female flower head

POLLEN AT ITS TIP
One of the male flower heads at the tip of this great pond sedge already has its stamens open and is shedding yellow pollen. The female flower heads are carried lower on the stem; these are not yet mature.

Common sedge

Reed grass

SEDGE AT THE EDGE
Beside the pond grows common sedge, its flower heads not quite fully opened as yet.

SPRING LILAC
Some of the earliest splashes of color around the pond are the pale lilac blooms of the cuckoo flower, or lady's-smock.

New spring growth

Lady's-smock

SEASON OF CATKINS
Willow trees, common on lake and river edges, greet spring with a fine display of furry catkins. These are the tree's flowers. Early bees and other insects visit the flowers for nectar and carry off the tree's pollen. The wind also blows pollen from the golden male catkins to the greenish female ones, which are usually borne on a different tree.

Female catkins

Goat (pussy) willow

Weeping willow

Female catkins

Crack willow

FLAGS STILL FURLED
The yellow flag iris will soon be in bloom. Here, the new leaves grow up from the thick, spreading, underground stem. From their swordlike shape this plant has gotten another name, the sword flag.

Yellow flag

Swordlike leaves

THE PUSS MOTH
The caterpillar of this moth feeds on the leaves of poplars and sallows (a kind of willow). Both trees grow in damp or moist soil, so puss moths and their caterpillars are often seen near ponds and rivers.

Male catkins covered in yellow pollen

Last year's stem

KING OF THE FLOWERS
The brilliant yellow flowers of the marsh marigold, or kingcup, decorate pond edges and other damp areas almost as soon as the snows melt away. A snail or some other plant-eater has already made a meal of one new leaf.

WATER PLANTAIN
A pale, woody stem is all that is left of last year's 3 ft (1 m) spray of flowers (p. 57). New leaves grow from a bulblike base. Despite its name, the water plantain is not one of the true plantains, enemy of all lawn gardeners.

New spring growth

Marsh marigold

Leaf damaged by snail

Meadow rue

Delicate, notched leaves

Water plantain

SPRING FLUSH
A young meadow rue bears its first flush of delicately notched leaves. It prefers damp' meadows and pond or stream banks.

Spring animals

As THE SPRING SUN'S WARMTH spreads through the water, animals begin to stir themselves from among the weeds and mud at the bottom of the pond. It is a time of urgent new life. Frogs and toads, fish and newts, are courting, mating, and laying eggs. Their offspring soon hatch in the warming water, eager to cash in on the spring burst of life that provides food for all. "Cold-blooded" aquatic creatures become more active with the rising water temperature, and in a mild spring the smaller ponds, which warm up faster than large ones, are soon seething with newborn snails, insects, amphibians, and many other creatures.

Frog spawn

Protective jelly surrounding egg

Black egg

THE SPAWN IS BORN
As early as January, adult frogs gather in ponds to mate and spawn, or lay eggs (pp. 38-39). Around March the female lays up to 3,000 eggs, fertilized by the male, who clings to her back. The water-absorbing jelly around each egg swells, and soon the whole mass is many times her body size.

BIG BROTHERS AND SISTERS
Tadpoles hatch from spawn some two to three weeks after laying. The warmer the water, the faster they develop. Here, common frog tadpoles from a large, cool pond, only two weeks out of their eggs, mingle with four-weekers from a small pond that warmed up more quickly.

Tiny tadpoles from a cool pond

Tadpoles from a warm pond

This engraving of a water flea shows its complex anatomy

BORN ONTO THEIR FOOD
Each adult pond snail lays up to 400 eggs, buried in a jelly-like "rope" attached to the underside of a submerged leaf on which the young snails will feed (p. 52).

Common toad

Dry, warty skin

A NEW LEAF
In spring, water snails lay their eggs under leaves like these water lily leaves.

Protective jelly

Snail eggs

Pond snails

Water fleas

Water lily leaves

SPRING BLOOM
Water fleas and other tiny animals and plants bring a pea-soup look to many ponds in spring. This is the early "bloom" of microorganisms that provides food for larger creatures.

TWO SEXES IN ONE
Many adult pond snails are hermaphrodites, having both male and female reproductive organs.

Damage to leaf edge caused by natural splitting

SECOND SPRING
This young water beetle, common in small ponds and ditches, may well be celebrating its second birthday. Two years ago it was an egg, in that autumn a larva, last spring a pupa, and last summer a newly emerged adult.

FIRST SPRING
A water beetle larva has large jaws ready to tackle and eat any small creature the spring pond has to offer. Some species stay as larvae for two years or more before changing into adults (p. 51).

KING OF THE BEETLES
The great diving beetle is the king of the carnivores in many small ponds, feeding on tadpoles, small fish, and almost anything else it can catch. In fact the dull, furrowed "back" (hard wing covers) on this one indicates it is not a king but a queen - a female. The male's wing cases are smooth and shiny.

Female beetles have furrowed wing covers

Pale-green fronds

SOME WEEKS TO TAKEOFF
A mayfly larva displays its characteristic three tails. Despite its name, this larva might become adult and fly off in April or June (p. 50).

Water beetle

Erpobdella leech

Water beetle larva

Mayfly larva

Water slater

Male newt

Crest along male's back

Female newt

Duckweed

LOOKING FOR A WORM
The erpobdella leech loops through the water in search of a meal. This leech does not suck blood, but attacks worms and other soft-bodied small creatures and swallows them whole.

FINDING A MATE
The female water slater piggybacks the male as he fertilizes the eggs, which she keeps in a pouch under her body.

BREEDING NEWTS
In spring the male newt develops a crest along his back and black spots over his skin. The female's skin remains olive-brown.

GREEN CEILING
In the spring sunshine, duckweed soon spreads across the pond (p. 44). The tiny fronds provide food for snails and insect larvae.

EARLY FLOWERS
The water crowfoot is an aquatic type of buttercup. The broad, flat leaves that float on the surface shade the water beneath, providing a good hiding place for fish.

Common frog

Smooth, shiny skin

Leaves that float on the surface are flat and broad

READY TO MATE
In spring, the male stickleback's throat and underside turn bright red (a red tinge can even be seen from above, as on the male shown here). In this breeding coloration, he entices the female to lay eggs in the nest he has built on the pond bed (p. 25).

ONE-YEAR-OLDS
In addition to breeding adults, spawn, and tadpoles, you may also find last year's babies around the pond in spring (pp. 38-41).

Frogs lose their tail soon after emerging

Leaves that grow under water are finely divided

Male stickleback

Female stickleback

Early summer plants

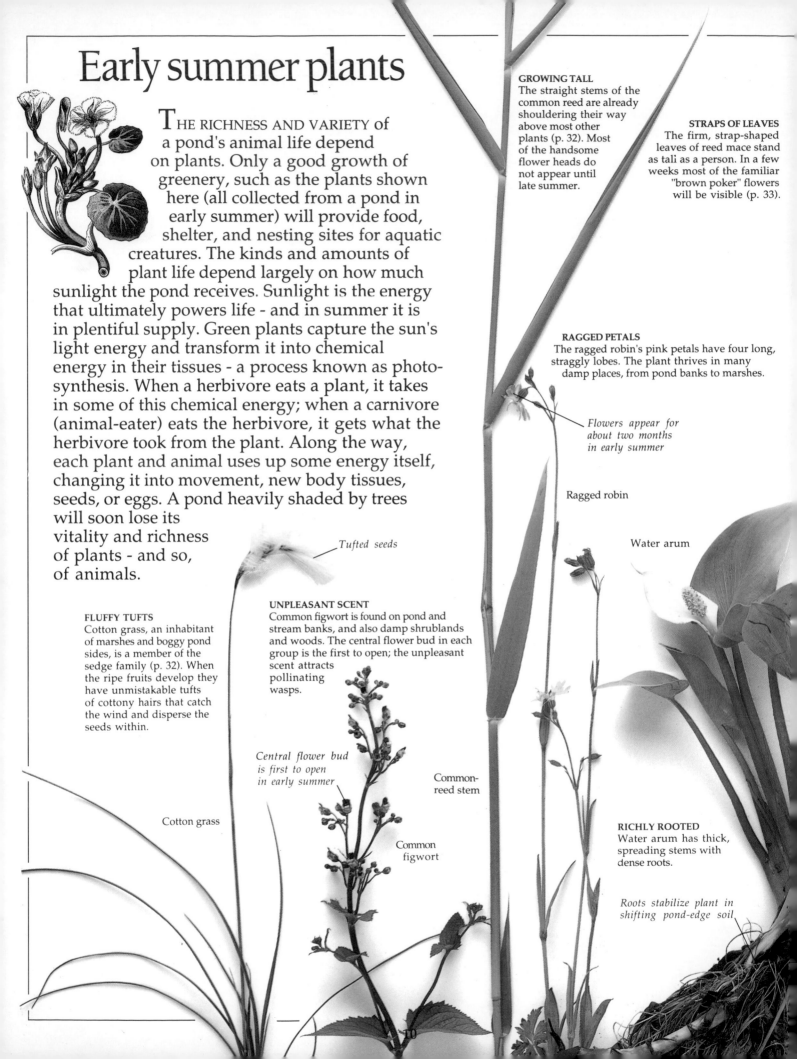

THE RICHNESS AND VARIETY of a pond's animal life depend on plants. Only a good growth of greenery, such as the plants shown here (all collected from a pond in early summer) will provide food, shelter, and nesting sites for aquatic creatures. The kinds and amounts of plant life depend largely on how much sunlight the pond receives. Sunlight is the energy that ultimately powers life - and in summer it is in plentiful supply. Green plants capture the sun's light energy and transform it into chemical energy in their tissues - a process known as photosynthesis. When a herbivore eats a plant, it takes in some of this chemical energy; when a carnivore (animal-eater) eats the herbivore, it gets what the herbivore took from the plant. Along the way, each plant and animal uses up some energy itself, changing it into movement, new body tissues, seeds, or eggs. A pond heavily shaded by trees will soon lose its vitality and richness of plants - and so, of animals.

GROWING TALL
The straight stems of the common reed are already shouldering their way above most other plants (p. 32). Most of the handsome flower heads do not appear until late summer.

STRAPS OF LEAVES
The firm, strap-shaped leaves of reed mace stand as tall as a person. In a few weeks most of the familiar "brown poker" flowers will be visible (p. 33).

RAGGED PETALS
The ragged robin's pink petals have four long, straggly lobes. The plant thrives in many damp places, from pond banks to marshes.

Flowers appear for about two months in early summer

Ragged robin

Water arum

Tufted seeds

FLUFFY TUFTS
Cotton grass, an inhabitant of marshes and boggy pond sides, is a member of the sedge family (p. 32). When the ripe fruits develop they have unmistakable tufts of cottony hairs that catch the wind and disperse the seeds within.

UNPLEASANT SCENT
Common figwort is found on pond and stream banks, and also damp shrublands and woods. The central flower bud in each group is the first to open; the unpleasant scent attracts pollinating wasps.

Central flower bud is first to open in early summer

Cotton grass

Common figwort

Common-reed stem

RICHLY ROOTED
Water arum has thick, spreading stems with dense roots.

Roots stabilize plant in shifting pond-edge soil

RIPENING FRUITS
The gray willow's leaves are more rounded than the spear-shaped leaves of the weeping willow. This tree, also called the sallow, is developing fluff-covered fruits from the female catkins (p. 7). Like most willows, it roots well in damp ground by ponds and rivers.

EMERGING FLOWERS
The yellow flowers of the yellow flag iris are just beginning to unfurl from their protective bracts (sheaths).

Reed mace

Female catkin _____

Fluffy fruits

SEDGE SEEDS
In summer the fuzzy yellowish flower heads of false fox sedge (p. 33) darken to ripe seeds ready to be scattered along the pond bank.

Gray willow

Bract

Style *Petal*

Sepal

Darkening seed heads

PETALS AND SEPALS
The "petals" of the yellow flag are, in fact, made up of sepals, petals, and styles (the female parts of the flower that help to receive the pollen).

Cone

False fox sedge

Yellow flag

CONE BEARER
The marsh horsetail grows best in very moist ground and shallow water. Horsetails do not bear flowers; instead they have conelike structures at their stem tips (compare with the mare's-tail on p. 12).

Marsh horsetail

Early summer animals

Early summer is a time of thinning out and fattening up for pond animals. The swarms of young tadpoles, insect larvae, and water snails feed greedily on the abundant plant growth of this season (pp. 10-11).

But they are gradually thinned out by larger predatory creatures, such as beetle larvae and dragonfly nymphs (p. 48), newts, and small fish. These grow fat and in their turn may be eaten by larger creatures, from frogs to fish, by visiting birds like herons, and perhaps by water shrew, mink, and other mammals. And so the food chain of the pond builds up: plants first, then herbivores (plant-eaters), to carnivores (meat-eaters). But this is not the end. Death comes to all and, when it does, creatures such as water slaters move in to consume plant and animal remains. Droppings of all creatures enrich the water, providing minerals and other raw materials for fresh plant growth. So the nutrients go around and around, being recycled in the miniature ecosystem that is the pond.

Silver water beetle, wing cases lifted to show wings

Common toad

GOOD-BYE FOR THIS YEAR
A few of the dozens of breeding toads may still be hanging around near the pond. But most have now gone to their favorite damp corners, in hedges, under logs, and among the undergrowth. They will not return to the pond until next spring.

PETAL-LESS FLOWERS
Mare's-tail is a shallow-water plant of ponds and streams. The numerous tiny pond creatures of this season squirm and swim around its stems. Where the leaves join the stem, it bears tiny flowers without petals.

Tadpoles with developing back legs

BACK LEGS FIRST
Frog tadpoles are now fewer in number; many of their siblings have been eaten by fish, newts, diving beetles, and dragonfly nymphs. They have their back legs, which appear after about seven weeks. This change in body shape, from tadpole to adult frog, is called "metamorphosis."

Great pond snail

GROWN UP
This great pond snail is nearing full size, about 2 in (5 cm) long. It slides slowly over the bottom of the pond, eating decaying plant remains.

Mare's-tail

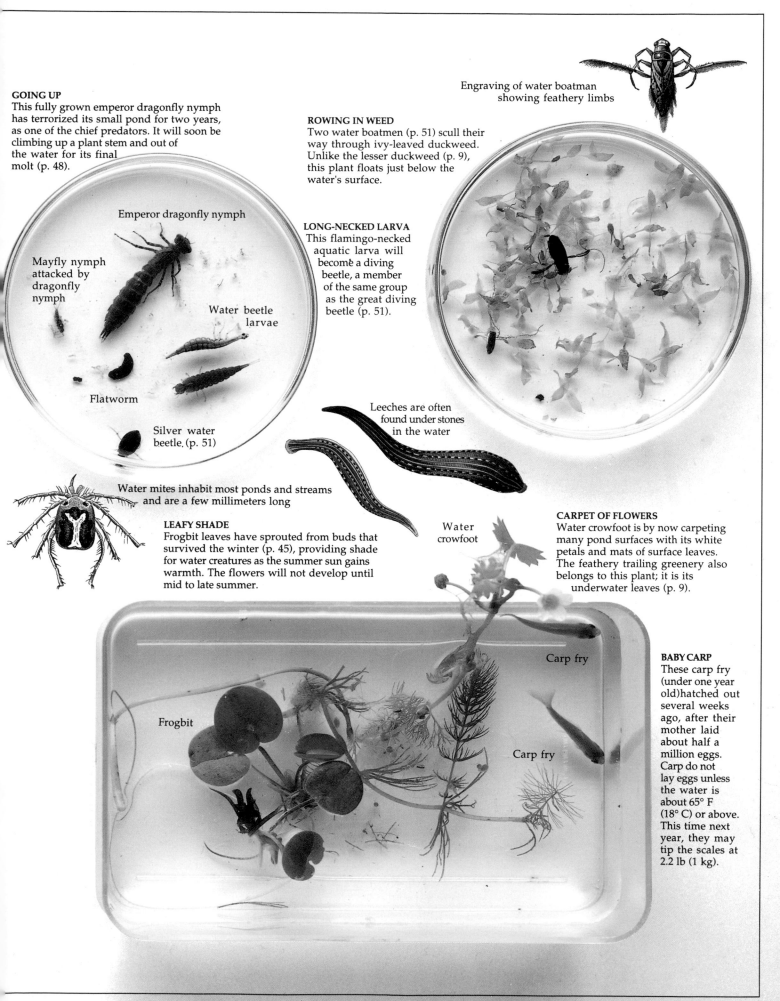

GOING UP
This fully grown emperor dragonfly nymph has terrorized its small pond for two years, as one of the chief predators. It will soon be climbing up a plant stem and out of the water for its final molt (p. 48).

Mayfly nymph attacked by dragonfly nymph

Emperor dragonfly nymph

Water beetle larvae

Flatworm

Silver water beetle. (p. 51)

ROWING IN WEED
Two water boatmen (p. 51) scull their way through ivy-leaved duckweed. Unlike the lesser duckweed (p. 9), this plant floats just below the water's surface.

LONG-NECKED LARVA
This flamingo-necked aquatic larva will become a diving beetle, a member of the same group as the great diving beetle (p. 51).

Engraving of water boatman showing feathery limbs

Leeches are often found under stones in the water

Water mites inhabit most ponds and streams and are a few millimeters long

LEAFY SHADE
Frogbit leaves have sprouted from buds that survived the winter (p. 45), providing shade for water creatures as the summer sun gains warmth. The flowers will not develop until mid to late summer.

Water crowfoot

CARPET OF FLOWERS
Water crowfoot is by now carpeting many pond surfaces with its white petals and mats of surface leaves. The feathery trailing greenery also belongs to this plant; it is its underwater leaves (p. 9).

Carp fry

Carp fry

Frogbit

BABY CARP
These carp fry (under one year old) hatched out several weeks ago, after their mother laid about half a million eggs. Carp do not lay eggs unless the water is about 65° F (18° C) or above. This time next year, they may tip the scales at 2.2 lb (1 kg).

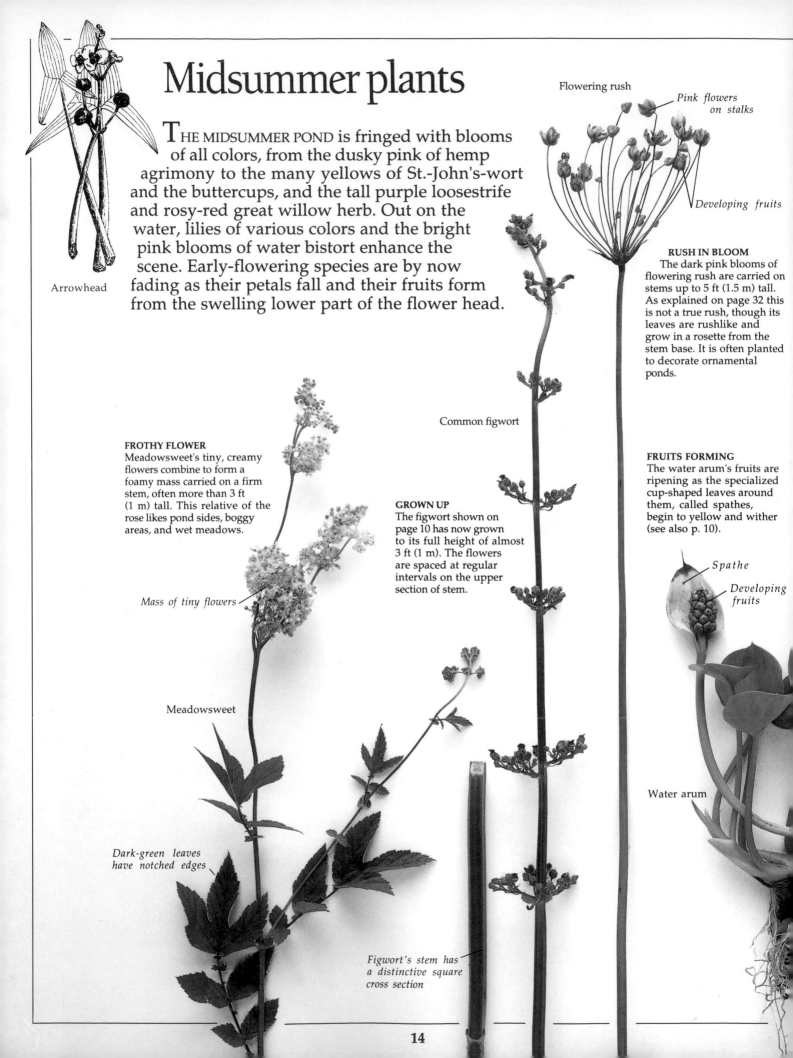

Midsummer plants

Arrowhead

THE MIDSUMMER POND is fringed with blooms of all colors, from the dusky pink of hemp agrimony to the many yellows of St.-John's-wort and the buttercups, and the tall purple loosestrife and rosy-red great willow herb. Out on the water, lilies of various colors and the bright pink blooms of water bistort enhance the scene. Early-flowering species are by now fading as their petals fall and their fruits form from the swelling lower part of the flower head.

Flowering rush

Pink flowers on stalks

Developing fruits

RUSH IN BLOOM
The dark pink blooms of flowering rush are carried on stems up to 5 ft (1.5 m) tall. As explained on page 32 this is not a true rush, though its leaves are rushlike and grow in a rosette from the stem base. It is often planted to decorate ornamental ponds.

Common figwort

FROTHY FLOWER
Meadowsweet's tiny, creamy flowers combine to form a foamy mass carried on a firm stem, often more than 3 ft (1 m) tall. This relative of the rose likes pond sides, boggy areas, and wet meadows.

GROWN UP
The figwort shown on page 10 has now grown to its full height of almost 3 ft (1 m). The flowers are spaced at regular intervals on the upper section of stem.

FRUITS FORMING
The water arum's fruits are ripening as the specialized cup-shaped leaves around them, called spathes, begin to yellow and wither (see also p. 10).

Spathe

Developing fruits

Mass of tiny flowers

Meadowsweet

Water arum

Dark-green leaves have notched edges

Figwort's stem has a distinctive square cross section

GRAYISH-GREEN SHEEN
Osier, a typically water-loving willow, has extremely long, sharply pointed leaves. The tiny hairs on the underside of each leaf give it a grayish-green sheen.

Osier

Hawthorn

Haw

Water plantain's small pinky-white flowers bloom on tall, erect sprays of stems at this time of year (p. 57)

Dark green upperside of leaf

Gray underside of leaf

GREEN TO RED
Hawthorns tolerate wide variations in soil type and moisture content, so this tree is often found growing by ponds. The green fruits are called "haws." In a few weeks the haws will turn a deep rich, red color and attract birds such as waxwings and tits to the pond side.

WITHERED PETALS
The bright blooms (p. 10) of the yellow flag iris have withered to brown, and the fruit capsules are now forming. Each capsule resembles a chunky pea pod and contains several knobbly seeds.

Seed pods

ST.-JOHN'S-WORT
This plant (see also p. 16) grows in damp places such as shady woods and pond banks. The flowers begin to fade in midsummer.

SPHERES AND SPEARS
Its yellow flower indicates that greater spearwort is a type of buttercup. Two round, spiky heads of ripening fruits are shown, as well as the spear-shaped leaves that give the plant its name.

Withered flower

St.-John's-wort

Ripening fruit

Yellow flag

PINK FORGET-ME-NOT
Water forget-me-not flowers throughout the summer, in damp and shady places. Its stems trail along the pond edge, and its flowers may be blue, white, or pink.

Spear-shaped leaves

Water forget-me-not

Greater spearwort

15

Midsummer animals

MIDSUMMER IS A TIME OF GROWTH and departure in the pond. The frantic spring and early-summer rush of new life is slowing down. The surviving youngsters of this year's eggs, now fewer in number, settle down to the serious business of growing, building up stores of fat in their bodies, and preparing for the shorter, colder days ahead. Frog and toad tadpoles have changed into air-breathing mini-adults, ready to leave the water and take their first hops on land. A few young newts may stay as tadpoles with gills through the coming autumn and winter, but others, now adult in shape, are also moving away. The departure from the pond continues as aquatic insect larvae of many kinds develop into adults (p. 50), from tiny gnats, midges, and mosquitoes to the mighty dragonflies (p. 48) that prey on them.

Tiny gnats (male and female) dance above the pond's surface during long summer evenings

Not rowing but flying, this water boatman shows its strong wings (p. 51)

Water snail

Growth rings

Toadlet

Newtlets

Gills

Toadlet

NEWTLETS
These young newts still have their gills to help absorb oxygen from the warm summer pond water. They hide among weeds, eating water fleas and other tiny creatures.

RINGS AND BANDS
Periods of slow growth are visible on this water snail's shell. They are the thin rings toward the opening which cross the spiral banding pattern.

TOADLETS
By now, toad tadpoles have grown their front legs and lost their tails, to resemble their parents. In midsummer they leave the pond for life on land.

HAPPY WANDERER
The wandering snail is more tolerant of water with fewer minerals (p. 52) than, for example, the great pond snail is - and so is more widespread in ponds and slow rivers.

SQUARE STEM
There are several species of St.-John's-wort (p. 15). This one is square-stemmed, and lines watersides, marshes, and damp shrubland.

BABY BIVALVES
In about 10 years, these young freshwater mollusks will be many times this size (p. 52). In their early years they are busy feeding and absorbing calcium from the water to build their shell.

Young freshwater molluscs

Wandering snails

Snail emerging from shell

Square-stemmed St.-John's-wort

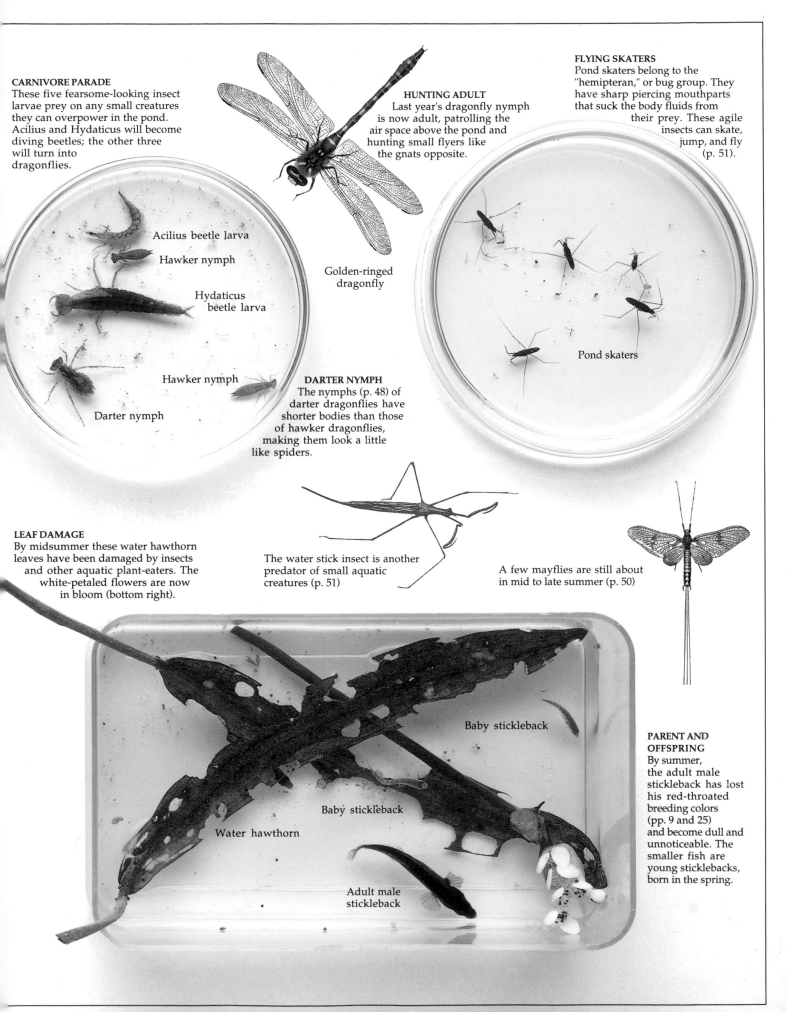

CARNIVORE PARADE
These five fearsome-looking insect larvae prey on any small creatures they can overpower in the pond. Acilius and Hydaticus will become diving beetles; the other three will turn into dragonflies.

HUNTING ADULT
Last year's dragonfly nymph is now adult, patrolling the air space above the pond and hunting small flyers like the gnats opposite.

FLYING SKATERS
Pond skaters belong to the "hemipteran," or bug group. They have sharp piercing mouthparts that suck the body fluids from their prey. These agile insects can skate, jump, and fly (p. 51).

Acilius beetle larva

Hawker nymph

Hydaticus beetle larva

Golden-ringed dragonfly

Hawker nymph

Darter nymph

DARTER NYMPH
The nymphs (p. 48) of darter dragonflies have shorter bodies than those of hawker dragonflies, making them look a little like spiders.

Pond skaters

LEAF DAMAGE
By midsummer these water hawthorn leaves have been damaged by insects and other aquatic plant-eaters. The white-petaled flowers are now in bloom (bottom right).

The water stick insect is another predator of small aquatic creatures (p. 51)

A few mayflies are still about in mid to late summer (p. 50)

Baby stickleback

Baby stickleback

Water hawthorn

Adult male stickleback

PARENT AND OFFSPRING
By summer, the adult male stickleback has lost his red-throated breeding colors (pp. 9 and 25) and become dull and unnoticeable. The smaller fish are young sticklebacks, born in the spring.

The pond in autumn

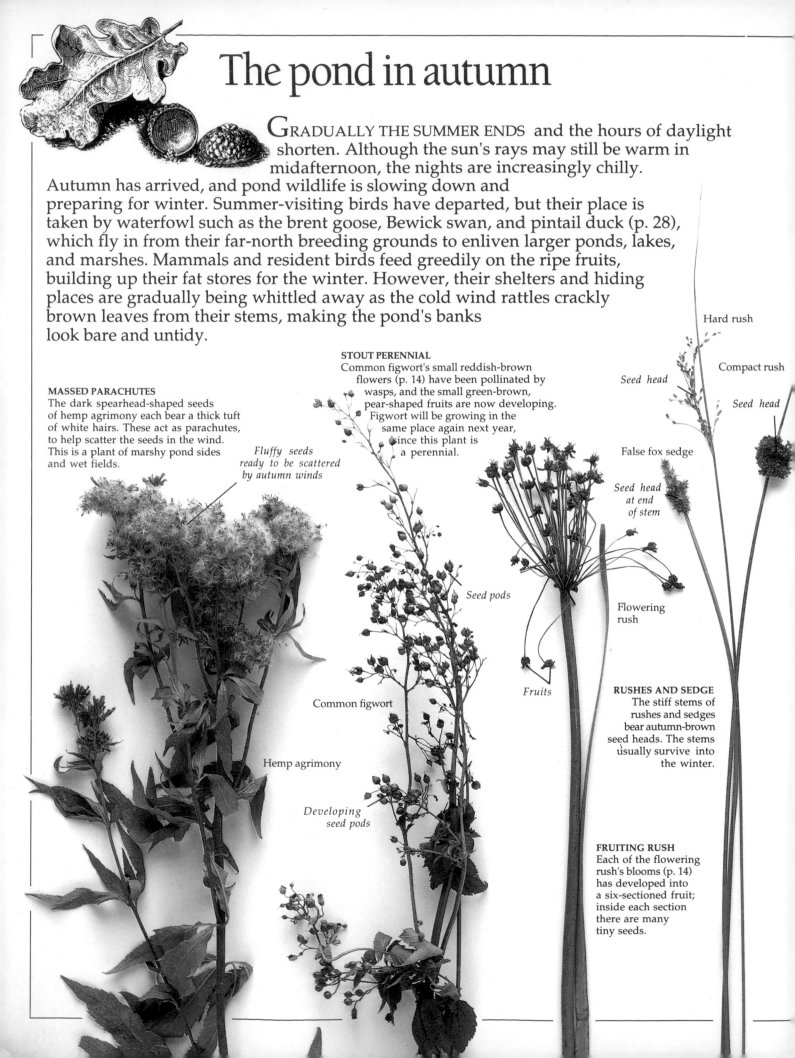

GRADUALLY THE SUMMER ENDS and the hours of daylight shorten. Although the sun's rays may still be warm in midafternoon, the nights are increasingly chilly. Autumn has arrived, and pond wildlife is slowing down and preparing for winter. Summer-visiting birds have departed, but their place is taken by waterfowl such as the brent goose, Bewick swan, and pintail duck (p. 28), which fly in from their far-north breeding grounds to enliven larger ponds, lakes, and marshes. Mammals and resident birds feed greedily on the ripe fruits, building up their fat stores for the winter. However, their shelters and hiding places are gradually being whittled away as the cold wind rattles crackly brown leaves from their stems, making the pond's banks look bare and untidy.

MASSED PARACHUTES
The dark spearhead-shaped seeds of hemp agrimony each bear a thick tuft of white hairs. These act as parachutes, to help scatter the seeds in the wind. This is a plant of marshy pond sides and wet fields.

Fluffy seeds ready to be scattered by autumn winds

STOUT PERENNIAL
Common figwort's small reddish-brown flowers (p. 14) have been pollinated by wasps, and the small green-brown, pear-shaped fruits are now developing. Figwort will be growing in the same place again next year, since this plant is a perennial.

Seed pods

Common figwort

Hemp agrimony

Developing seed pods

Hard rush

Compact rush

Seed head

Seed head

False fox sedge

Seed head at end of stem

Fruits

Flowering rush

RUSHES AND SEDGE
The stiff stems of rushes and sedges bear autumn-brown seed heads. The stems usually survive into the winter.

FRUITING RUSH
Each of the flowering rush's blooms (p. 14) has developed into a six-sectioned fruit; inside each section there are many tiny seeds.

WINTER POKER
Reed mace's familiar brown "poker" of seeds stands guard over marshes and ponds, usually throughout the winter. In spring the poker bursts to scatter the fluffy-haired seeds.

Brown "poker" full of seeds

SNAILS SLOWING DOWN
Falling water temperatures mean that even pond snails begin to move around more slowly, tending to stay in deeper water.

Pond snails

Caddis fly cases

Alder cones

Reed mace

Newtlet

Dragonfly nymph

ALDER "CONES"
In autumn the alder's green fruits ripen to a brown-black color and stay on the tree during winter. They are sometimes mistaken for small pine cones, but the alder is not a conifer. It prefers pond banks and the sides of streams, and its light seeds drop onto the water and float to new ground.

Alder

Seed pods

HOME IN A TUBE
Rectangular leaf fragments stuck into a spiral pattern and curled into a tube signal the larval case of the great red sedge, a type of caddis fly (p. 50). These larvae will emerge as adult flies next year.

NEXT YEAR'S ADULT
Dragonfly nymphs found in the pond at this time of year will survive the winter and emerge next year.

RECYCLING FUNGI
Animal and plant corpses are digested by fungi, and their nutrients are recycled. Here, an old pond-side tree was attacked and weakened by bracket fungi.

Yellow flag

AUTUMN JUVENILE
A young common newt, still equipped with gills, will spend the winter as a "juvenile" and finish its change into an adult next year.

Bracket fungi grow on the outside of the trunk

ON THE BOTTOM
Leaves, twigs, and other debris blow into the pond or are washed in by heavy autumn rains. This heap of debris, lying over the mud of the pond bed, will shelter all kinds of small water creatures during the winter months.

SOON TO SET SEED
The seed capsules of the yellow flag iris are now thick with ripening brown seeds (compare the same "pods" on p. 15). Eventually the fleshy capsule walls dry out and split into three boat-shaped segments; these peel back to release the seeds.

Oak leaf

Willow leaf

Birch leaf

Willow twigs

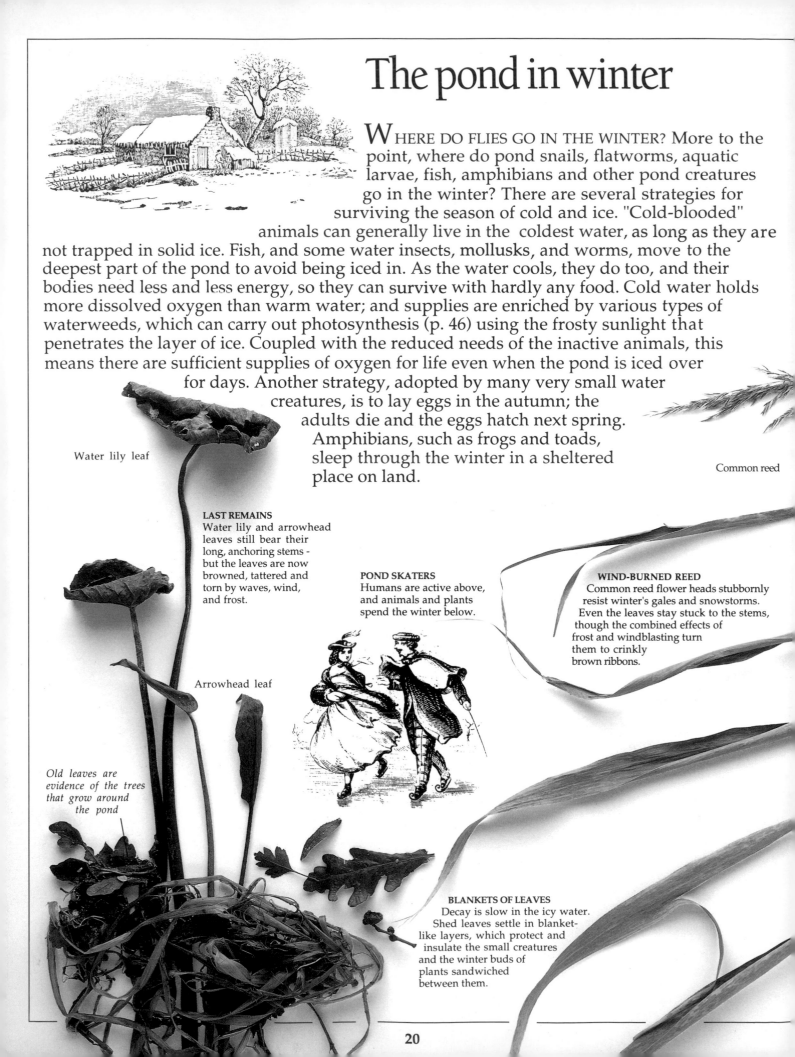

The pond in winter

WHERE DO FLIES GO IN THE WINTER? More to the point, where do pond snails, flatworms, aquatic larvae, fish, amphibians and other pond creatures go in the winter? There are several strategies for surviving the season of cold and ice. "Cold-blooded" animals can generally live in the coldest water, as long as they are not trapped in solid ice. Fish, and some water insects, mollusks, and worms, move to the deepest part of the pond to avoid being iced in. As the water cools, they do too, and their bodies need less and less energy, so they can survive with hardly any food. Cold water holds more dissolved oxygen than warm water; and supplies are enriched by various types of waterweeds, which can carry out photosynthesis (p. 46) using the frosty sunlight that penetrates the layer of ice. Coupled with the reduced needs of the inactive animals, this means there are sufficient supplies of oxygen for life even when the pond is iced over for days. Another strategy, adopted by many very small water creatures, is to lay eggs in the autumn; the adults die and the eggs hatch next spring. Amphibians, such as frogs and toads, sleep through the winter in a sheltered place on land.

Water lily leaf

Common reed

LAST REMAINS
Water lily and arrowhead leaves still bear their long, anchoring stems - but the leaves are now browned, tattered and torn by waves, wind, and frost.

POND SKATERS
Humans are active above, and animals and plants spend the winter below.

WIND-BURNED REED
Common reed flower heads stubbornly resist winter's gales and snowstorms. Even the leaves stay stuck to the stems, though the combined effects of frost and windblasting turn them to crinkly brown ribbons.

Arrowhead leaf

Old leaves are evidence of the trees that grow around the pond

BLANKETS OF LEAVES
Decay is slow in the icy water. Shed leaves settle in blanket-like layers, which protect and insulate the small creatures and the winter buds of plants sandwiched between them.

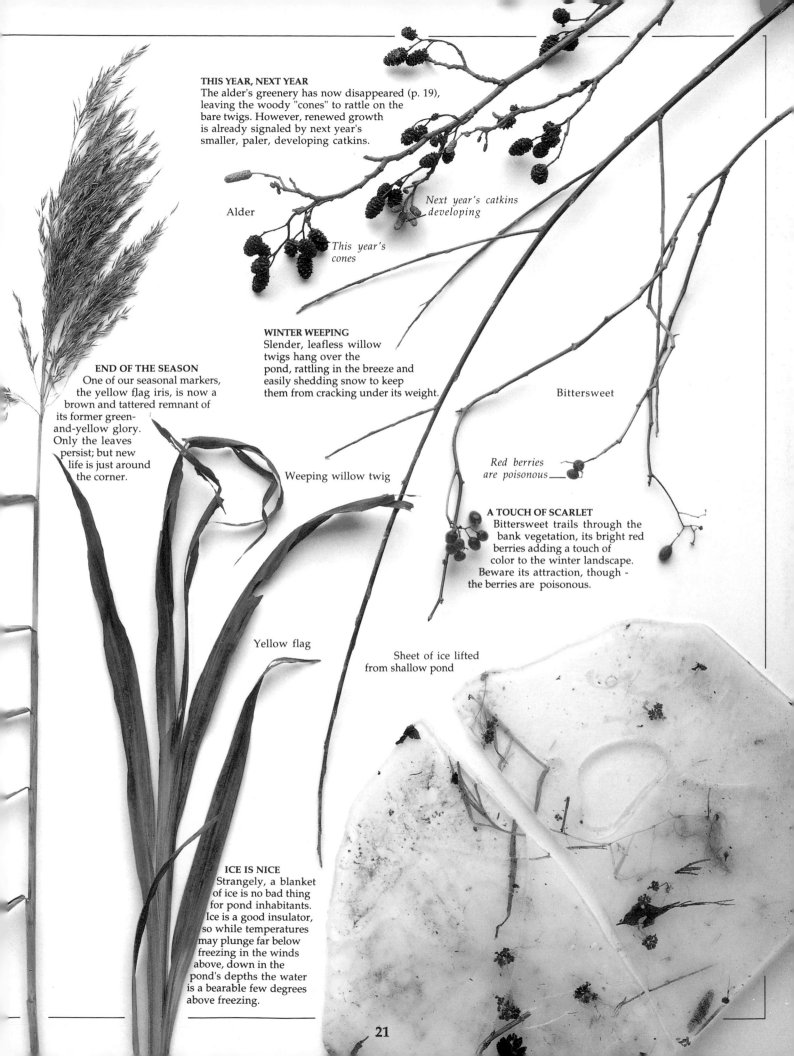

THIS YEAR, NEXT YEAR
The alder's greenery has now disappeared (p. 19), leaving the woody "cones" to rattle on the bare twigs. However, renewed growth is already signaled by next year's smaller, paler, developing catkins.

Alder

Next year's catkins developing

This year's cones

WINTER WEEPING
Slender, leafless willow twigs hang over the pond, rattling in the breeze and easily shedding snow to keep them from cracking under its weight.

Bittersweet

END OF THE SEASON
One of our seasonal markers, the yellow flag iris, is now a brown and tattered remnant of its former green-and-yellow glory. Only the leaves persist; but new life is just around the corner.

Weeping willow twig

Red berries are poisonous

A TOUCH OF SCARLET
Bittersweet trails through the bank vegetation, its bright red berries adding a touch of color to the winter landscape. Beware its attraction, though - the berries are poisonous.

Yellow flag

Sheet of ice lifted from shallow pond

ICE IS NICE
Strangely, a blanket of ice is no bad thing for pond inhabitants. Ice is a good insulator, so while temperatures may plunge far below freezing in the winds above, down in the pond's depths the water is a bearable few degrees above freezing.

21

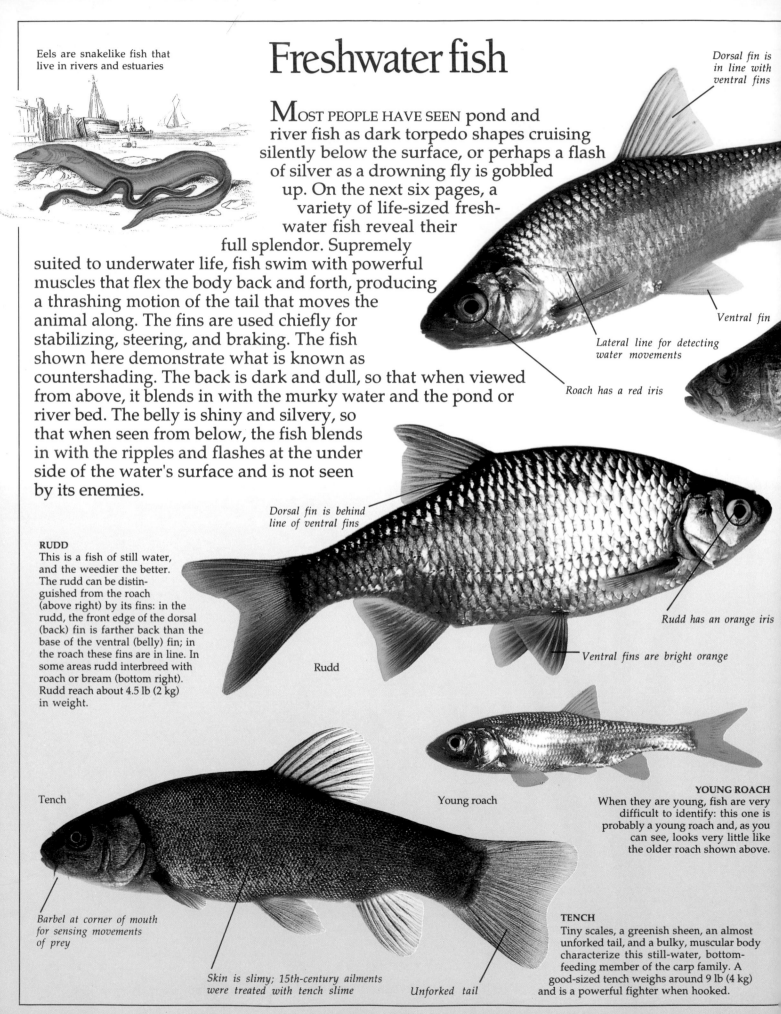

Eels are snakelike fish that live in rivers and estuaries

Freshwater fish

MOST PEOPLE HAVE SEEN pond and river fish as dark torpedo shapes cruising silently below the surface, or perhaps a flash of silver as a drowning fly is gobbled up. On the next six pages, a variety of life-sized freshwater fish reveal their full splendor. Supremely suited to underwater life, fish swim with powerful muscles that flex the body back and forth, producing a thrashing motion of the tail that moves the animal along. The fins are used chiefly for stabilizing, steering, and braking. The fish shown here demonstrate what is known as countershading. The back is dark and dull, so that when viewed from above, it blends in with the murky water and the pond or river bed. The belly is shiny and silvery, so that when seen from below, the fish blends in with the ripples and flashes at the under side of the water's surface and is not seen by its enemies.

Dorsal fin is in line with ventral fins

Ventral fin

Lateral line for detecting water movements

Roach has a red iris

RUDD
This is a fish of still water, and the weedier the better. The rudd can be distinguished from the roach (above right) by its fins: in the rudd, the front edge of the dorsal (back) fin is farther back than the base of the ventral (belly) fin; in the roach these fins are in line. In some areas rudd interbreed with roach or bream (bottom right). Rudd reach about 4.5 lb (2 kg) in weight.

Dorsal fin is behind line of ventral fins

Rudd has an orange iris

Ventral fins are bright orange

Rudd

Tench

Young roach

YOUNG ROACH
When they are young, fish are very difficult to identify: this one is probably a young roach and, as you can see, looks very little like the older roach shown above.

Barbel at corner of mouth for sensing movements of prey

Skin is slimy; 15th-century ailments were treated with tench slime

Unforked tail

TENCH
Tiny scales, a greenish sheen, an almost unforked tail, and a bulky, muscular body characterize this still-water, bottom-feeding member of the carp family. A good-sized tench weighs around 9 lb (4 kg) and is a powerful fighter when hooked.

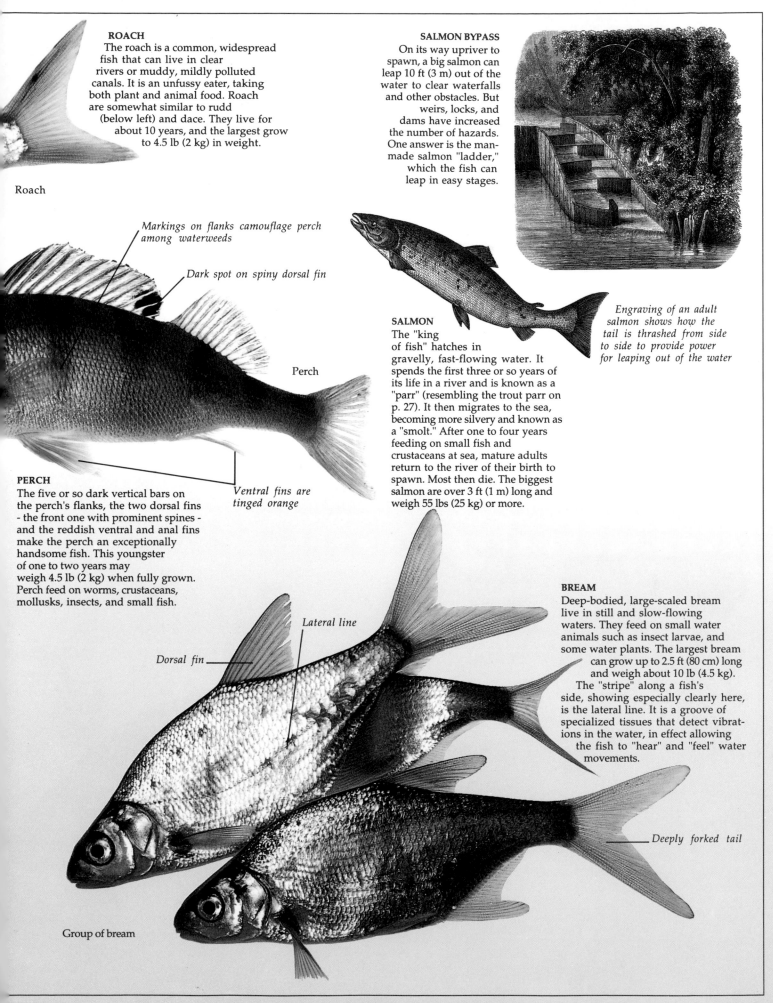

ROACH
The roach is a common, widespread fish that can live in clear rivers or muddy, mildly polluted canals. It is an unfussy eater, taking both plant and animal food. Roach are somewhat similar to rudd (below left) and dace. They live for about 10 years, and the largest grow to 4.5 lb (2 kg) in weight.

Roach

SALMON BYPASS
On its way upriver to spawn, a big salmon can leap 10 ft (3 m) out of the water to clear waterfalls and other obstacles. But weirs, locks, and dams have increased the number of hazards. One answer is the man-made salmon "ladder," which the fish can leap in easy stages.

Markings on flanks camouflage perch among waterweeds

Dark spot on spiny dorsal fin

Perch

SALMON
The "king of fish" hatches in gravelly, fast-flowing water. It spends the first three or so years of its life in a river and is known as a "parr" (resembling the trout parr on p. 27). It then migrates to the sea, becoming more silvery and known as a "smolt." After one to four years feeding on small fish and crustaceans at sea, mature adults return to the river of their birth to spawn. Most then die. The biggest salmon are over 3 ft (1 m) long and weigh 55 lbs (25 kg) or more.

Engraving of an adult salmon shows how the tail is thrashed from side to side to provide power for leaping out of the water

PERCH
The five or so dark vertical bars on the perch's flanks, the two dorsal fins - the front one with prominent spines - and the reddish ventral and anal fins make the perch an exceptionally handsome fish. This youngster of one to two years may weigh 4.5 lb (2 kg) when fully grown. Perch feed on worms, crustaceans, mollusks, insects, and small fish.

Ventral fins are tinged orange

BREAM
Deep-bodied, large-scaled bream live in still and slow-flowing waters. They feed on small water animals such as insect larvae, and some water plants. The largest bream can grow up to 2.5 ft (80 cm) long and weigh about 10 lb (4.5 kg). The "stripe" along a fish's side, showing especially clearly here, is the lateral line. It is a groove of specialized tissues that detect vibrations in the water, in effect allowing the fish to "hear" and "feel" water movements.

Lateral line

Dorsal fin

Deeply forked tail

Group of bream

Distinctive markings make these fish highly prized

Koi carp

Mouth can be extended to suck up food from pond bottom

Barbel on side of mouth

KOI CARP

People in Japan and China have been breeding carp for hundreds of years. The koi is a cultivated variety of fish belonging to the same group as the common carp. It is known in Japan as Nishiki Koi, or Brocaded Carp. Koi have been bred for their color and patterning as well as for size - some grow to over 3 ft (1 m) long. They have been stocked in ponds and lakes across Europe and North America, and prized specimens are extremely valuable.

PIKE AND EEL

An account from the 1880s describes a pike of some 10 lb (4.5 kg) that attempted to swallow an eel weighing almost as much. The eel tried to wriggle out through the pike's gills, the pike bit it in two, and both perished. Although the truth of this story is a little doubtful, it illustrates the voracious nature of the pike, a sleek predator with a mouthful of sharp teeth, and shows the toughness of the eel, which wriggles furiously and throws off slime when in trouble. Female eels grow to 3 ft (1 m) long and weigh around 4.5 lb (2 kg); males may be half this size.

Large, reflecting scales

Mirror carp

MIRROR CARP

Another form of common carp is the mirror carp, so named from the unusually large, shiny scales. These may occur down the side of the body (sometimes following the lateral line), and perhaps along the back, or scattered at random. Like other carp it feeds on the bottom, consuming small aquatic creatures and water plants. It reaches weights of up to 20 lb (9 kg).

Parts of the body have no scales

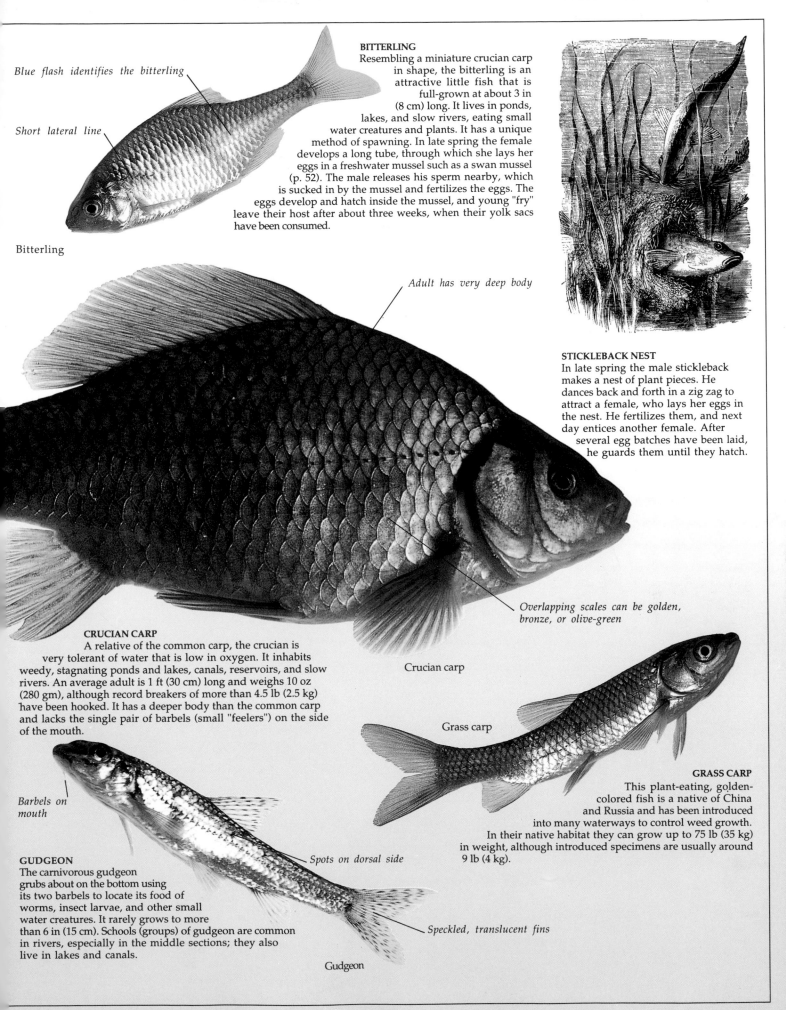

Blue flash identifies the bitterling

Short lateral line

BITTERLING
Resembling a miniature crucian carp in shape, the bitterling is an attractive little fish that is full-grown at about 3 in (8 cm) long. It lives in ponds, lakes, and slow rivers, eating small water creatures and plants. It has a unique method of spawning. In late spring the female develops a long tube, through which she lays her eggs in a freshwater mussel such as a swan mussel (p. 52). The male releases his sperm nearby, which is sucked in by the mussel and fertilizes the eggs. The eggs develop and hatch inside the mussel, and young "fry" leave their host after about three weeks, when their yolk sacs have been consumed.

Bitterling

Adult has very deep body

STICKLEBACK NEST
In late spring the male stickleback makes a nest of plant pieces. He dances back and forth in a zig zag to attract a female, who lays her eggs in the nest. He fertilizes them, and next day entices another female. After several egg batches have been laid, he guards them until they hatch.

Overlapping scales can be golden, bronze, or olive-green

Crucian carp

Grass carp

CRUCIAN CARP
A relative of the common carp, the crucian is very tolerant of water that is low in oxygen. It inhabits weedy, stagnating ponds and lakes, canals, reservoirs, and slow rivers. An average adult is 1 ft (30 cm) long and weighs 10 oz (280 gm), although record breakers of more than 4.5 lb (2.5 kg) have been hooked. It has a deeper body than the common carp and lacks the single pair of barbels (small "feelers") on the side of the mouth.

Barbels on mouth

GUDGEON
The carnivorous gudgeon grubs about on the bottom using its two barbels to locate its food of worms, insect larvae, and other small water creatures. It rarely grows to more than 6 in (15 cm). Schools (groups) of gudgeon are common in rivers, especially in the middle sections; they also live in lakes and canals.

Spots on dorsal side

GRASS CARP
This plant-eating, golden-colored fish is a native of China and Russia and has been introduced into many waterways to control weed growth. In their native habitat they can grow up to 75 lb (35 kg) in weight, although introduced specimens are usually around 9 lb (4 kg).

Speckled, translucent fins

Gudgeon

The trout

FEW FRESHWATER FISH match the trout for natural beauty and grace, for fighting power when hooked - and for taste when cooked! Trout belong to the salmon family. The brown trout and the sea trout are, in fact, different forms of the same species. The brown trout lives all its life in fresh water; the sea trout feeds in the sea and enters its home stream in summer, to breed in autumn. Adult brown trout may reach 3 ft (1 m) in length; sea trout can be half as long again. There are many variations between these two forms, telling them apart is difficult, because sea trout darken when they have been in fresh water for a few weeks and look like brown trout. In any case, trout differ greatly in appearance, depending on where they live, the nature of the water, the type of stream or lake bed, and the food they eat. Rainbow trout are another trout species altogether.

TYPICAL TROUT COUNTRY
An ideal trout stream - clear and cool running water, high in dissolved oxygen, with a gravelly bed for spawning. Trout are also found in clean lakes, usually in the shallows near their food.

Lateral line

Movements of the very mobile pectoral fins enable the fish to swim upward or downward

STREAMLINED PREDATOR
Brown trout, like other trout, are carnivorous. Food varies from tiny water fleas, flies, aquatic insect larvae (such as caddis larvae) and freshwater shrimps, to shellfish and other mollusks. The big brown trout, from large, deep lakes, prey on other fish such as char or whitefish.

Brown trout

COLORS OF THE RAINBOW
Rainbow trout were originally found in western North America (especially California). Like the brown trout, there are sea, lake, and river forms. Their eggs were brought to Europe in the 1900s, and these fish have since been introduced into many rivers, reservoirs, and lakes to provide sport and food. Rainbow trout breed in some large reservoirs, but rivers have to be regularly stocked with young produced in hatcheries (trout farms). The rainbow trout can live in warmer, less oxygenated water than the brown trout, so they are stocked in small lakes and large ponds where the brown trout would probably not survive.

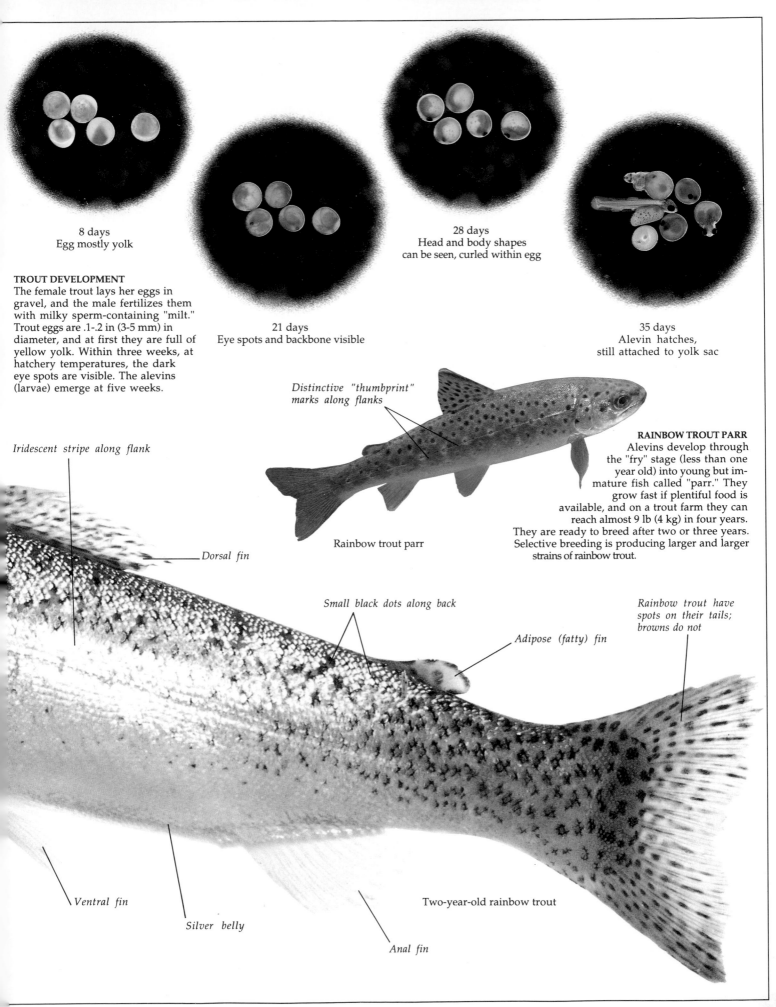

8 days
Egg mostly yolk

21 days
Eye spots and backbone visible

28 days
Head and body shapes
can be seen, curled within egg

35 days
Alevin hatches,
still attached to yolk sac

TROUT DEVELOPMENT
The female trout lays her eggs in
gravel, and the male fertilizes them
with milky sperm-containing "milt."
Trout eggs are .1-.2 in (3-5 mm) in
diameter, and at first they are full of
yellow yolk. Within three weeks, at
hatchery temperatures, the dark
eye spots are visible. The alevins
(larvae) emerge at five weeks.

*Distinctive "thumbprint"
marks along flanks*

RAINBOW TROUT PARR
Alevins develop through
the "fry" stage (less than one
year old) into young but immature fish called "parr." They
grow fast if plentiful food is
available, and on a trout farm they can
reach almost 9 lb (4 kg) in four years.
They are ready to breed after two or three years.
Selective breeding is producing larger and larger
strains of rainbow trout.

Rainbow trout parr

Iridescent stripe along flank

Dorsal fin

Small black dots along back

Adipose (fatty) fin

*Rainbow trout have
spots on their tails;
browns do not*

Ventral fin

Silver belly

Anal fin

Two-year-old rainbow trout

Waterfowl

Water and its resident wildlife attract an amazing variety of birds. Quite at home on ponds, lakes, and rivers (as well as seashores) across the world are about 150 species of wildfowl, including swans, geese, and ducks. These generally heavy-bodied birds have webbed feet for swimming and long, flexible necks for dabbling in the water and rummaging in the muddy bed for food. During spring, dense plant growth on the bank provides many species with safe and sheltered nesting sites. In summer, the proud parents can be seen leading their fluffy chicks across the water. Aquatic plants and animals are a ready source of food for most of the year. In winter, when ponds freeze over, many wildfowl retreat to parks and gardens where they feast on scraps donated by well-wishing humans. Others fly south, often covering vast distances to find a more favorable climate in which to spend the winter.

Eider duck nest and eggs

Soft down feathers insulate the eggs in the nest

Teal nest and eggs

SPECIALLY GROWN DOWN
Ultra-soft eiderdown feathers grow on the female eider duck's breast. She plucks them to cocoon her eggs as she nests on seashore, lake shore or riverbank.

TEAL NEST
The teal makes its nest in dense undergrowth. The female is very careful when visiting her chicks, so as not to attract predators.

TUFTED DUCK EGG
The six to 14 eggs are laid in a nest close to the water's edge. The chick hatches after 25 days in the egg, and within a day it is swimming.

28

Teal, one of the
smallest ducks

*Nest would be
lined with down
when being used*

ON THE WING
All wildfowl are strong
flyers, many covering
vast distances during
their annual migration.

Pintail
wing

ECLIPSE
Out of the breeding season,
the pintail drake molts to
his unnoticeable "eclipse"
plumage, which looks like the
female's coloring.

MALE AND FEMALE
In the breeding
season, most male
ducks, like the pintail
(far right), have bright
plumage to catch the
female's eye. The
female (right) is duller,
for camouflage on the nest.

Tufted duck

PARTIAL TO MUSSELS
The tufted duck feeds on freshwater
mussels, as well as small fish, frogs,
and insects.

Tufted duck
skull

MUSCOVY DUCK
This native of Central and South
American ponds and marshes has
a broad bill that scoops up aquatic
plants and animals alike.

Muscovy duck

Muscovy duck
skull

BEWARE THE ORANGE BILL
The mute swan's bill is usually covered by an
orange sheath. Male swans can be extremely
vicious, particularly in the breeding season when
defending their territory.

Swan

Vane

Quill

Flight feathers

*The broad bill shape is
suitable for dabbling
for plants in the water*

FROM THE MOLT
Water-dwelling birds depend on
their feathers to keep them dry
and much time is spent
preening to keep the feathers
in good condition.

Mute swan skull

Water birds

A STRETCH OF WATER acts as a magnet for all types of bird life. Many species, from sparrows to pheasants, come to drink. Others come to feed, from the tall, elegant heron that stands motionless as it watches for prey, to the flash of shimmering blue that signifies a kingfisher diving for its dinner. Bank plants, floating and submerged waterweeds, fish, frogs, insect larvae, shellfish, and other aquatic life provide food for many birds. Some species, like reed buntings and warblers, find security in the dense reed beds and waterside vegetation. Here they nest and raise their chicks, safe from predators such as foxes and hawks.

Kingfisher wing

Kingfisher

THE EXPERT FISHER
The brilliantly colored kingfisher dives from its favorite perch for fish, tadpoles, and shellfish. The sword-shaped bill is ideal for stabbing or spearing fish, then holding the slippery prey until it can be beaten into stillness on a branch and swallowed headfirst.

The white eggs have a glossy surface

Kingfisher eggs

WHITE EGGS
Kingfishers nest in a streambank burrow up to 3 ft (1 m) long, so their eggs are white - there is no need for camouflaging colors.

KINGFISHER WING AND TAIL
The electric colors act as a warning to predatory birds, advertising that the flesh is foul-tasting.

Tail and wing markings vary from species to species

Kingfisher tail

Short wings beat rapidly when flying

Kingfisher skull

Sharp bill for stabbing fish

Long, sharp bill for spearing fish

Heron skull

Heron

LONG AND LANKY
Herons inhabit ponds, marshes, and rivers, stalking fish and frogs in the shallows.

HERON'S HARPOON
The heron's fearsome bill makes an excellent fish-stabbing spear. This bird stands patiently until prey comes within reach, then darts out its long neck, stabs the victim, tosses it around, and swallows it whole.

Bittern skull

BITTERN
This bird points its bill skyward and sways with the reeds to avoid detection. It can also climb up reed stems. The bittern builds a shallow platform of reed leaves and stalks hidden deep in the reed beds. The five to six eggs take four weeks to hatch.

STEALTHY STALKER
The bittern is a solitary, daytime feeder, using its pointed beak to catch frogs, small fish, and insects.

Reed warbler
nest

Reed warbler

*Nest is made from reed
flower heads and
other vegetation*

*Nest is woven
round reed stalks*

SNIPE EGG
The coloring
camouflages the eggs
in the nest of this
small wading bird.

LITTLE GREBE EGG
White when laid,
eggs get discolored
by plants and mud.
The little grebe is
also known as the
"dabchick."

WATER RAIL EGG
Water rails are shy
birds of waterside
undergrowth. There
can be as many as
15 eggs in a clutch.

HERON EGG
The blue eggs are laid
in well-defended nests
built of sticks and
twigs.

Reed bunting

FINE RUSHWORK
The reed bunting's nest is
built by the female alone,
but both parents feed
the chicks on insects and
their larvae.

*The nest is made of
grasses and moss*

Reed bunting nest

DEEP CUP
The reed warbler's nest
is supported by several
stems, usually of
common reed. Its cup is
extra-deep, so that the
eggs and chicks do not
fall out when high
winds blow the reeds
over at an angle.

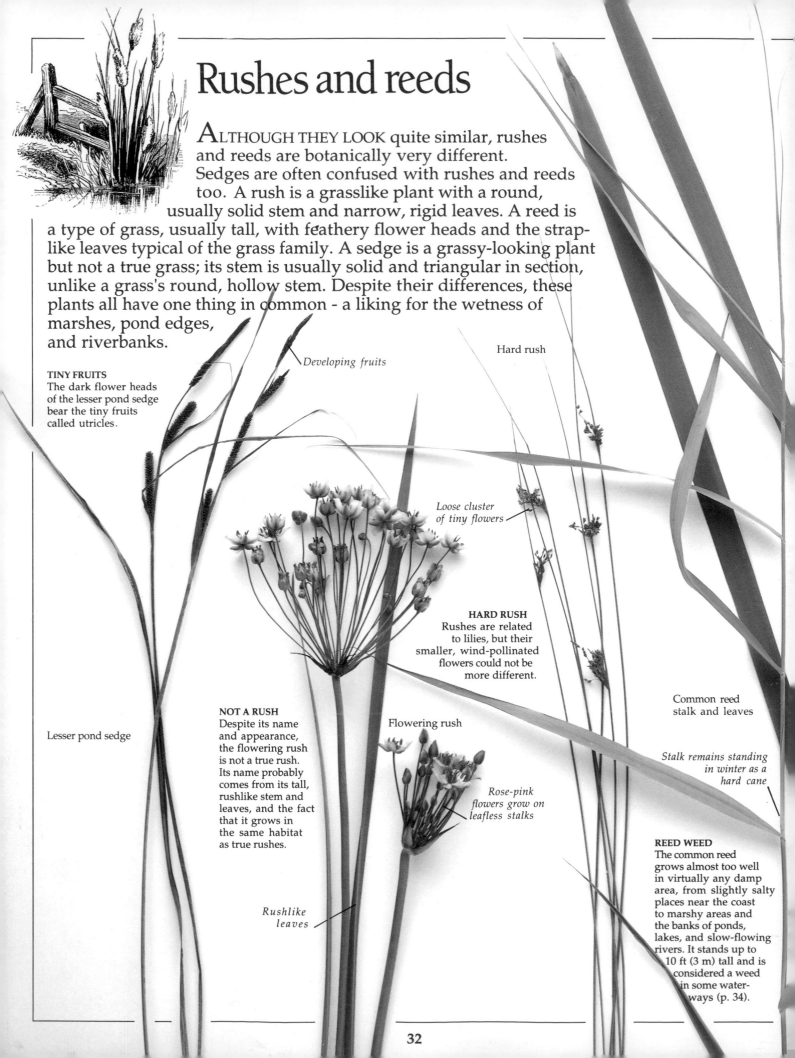

Rushes and reeds

ALTHOUGH THEY LOOK quite similar, rushes and reeds are botanically very different. Sedges are often confused with rushes and reeds too. A rush is a grasslike plant with a round, usually solid stem and narrow, rigid leaves. A reed is a type of grass, usually tall, with feathery flower heads and the strap-like leaves typical of the grass family. A sedge is a grassy-looking plant but not a true grass; its stem is usually solid and triangular in section, unlike a grass's round, hollow stem. Despite their differences, these plants all have one thing in common - a liking for the wetness of marshes, pond edges, and riverbanks.

Developing fruits

Hard rush

TINY FRUITS
The dark flower heads of the lesser pond sedge bear the tiny fruits called utricles.

Loose cluster of tiny flowers

HARD RUSH
Rushes are related to lilies, but their smaller, wind-pollinated flowers could not be more different.

Common reed stalk and leaves

Lesser pond sedge

NOT A RUSH
Despite its name and appearance, the flowering rush is not a true rush. Its name probably comes from its tall, rushlike stem and leaves, and the fact that it grows in the same habitat as true rushes.

Flowering rush

Stalk remains standing in winter as a hard cane

Rose-pink flowers grow on leafless stalks

REED WEED
The common reed grows almost too well in virtually any damp area, from slightly salty places near the coast to marshy areas and the banks of ponds, lakes, and slow-flowing rivers. It stands up to 10 ft (3 m) tall and is considered a weed in some water-ways (p. 34).

Rushlike leaves

Male flowers release clouds of pollen

Female flowers are fertilized by wind-carried pollen from male flowers, and fluffy seeds are released when the flower head splits open

Great reed mace

Ten to 20 male flower heads

Branched bur reed

Two to four female flower heads

Male and female flowers in the same flower head

False fox sedge

BRANCHING OUT
Each stem of branched bur reed bears both male and female flowers. The smaller, ball-shaped ones toward the tip are male; the female ones are larger and spiky, like a rolled-up hedgehog.

Triangular stem has sharp edges if rubbed downward

FALSE FOX SEDGE
On top of sharp-edged stems sit the tufty, yellow-green flower heads containing both male and female flowers.

TWO HEADS IN ONE
The great reed mace's poker-shaped flower head is in two parts. Above are hundreds of golden pollen-bearing male organs, and below are thousands of tiny female flowers packed into the brown cigar shape. The whole resembles the mace, a weapon of 15th-century knights, hence the name. The plant is commonly, but wrongly, called the bulrush, after the paintings of Moses in the bulrushes (p. 35).

Branched bur reed

Flower stalk

Bract at base of each branch of flower stalk

33

The reed bed

THE REED BED IS THE SILENT INVADER OF OPEN WATER. Dense growths of tall, marsh-ground plants, such as reed mace and common reed, spread around the pond's edge by thick underground rhizomes (stems). These grow sideways through the mud toward the water and send up fresh shoots at intervals. They spread into the shallows, pushing aside water lilies and mare's-tails. The reed stems slow the movement of water and trap particles carried by the current. At the end of each season the old leaves, stems, and fruits add to the growing tangle. In a few years, previously open water can be turned into thickly vegetated marsh. Some years later the reed bed has moved on, still swallowing up the shallows, and drier-ground plants such as osiers and sallows (types of willow) have moved in at the back of the bed. This conversion of water to land by characteristic stages is an example of "ecological succession."

Fool's watercress

WATER TO DRY LAND
Shown below are characteristic plants of pond and lake edge, with sallows and sedges higher up the shore, reed beds toward the middle, and mare's-tails and long-stemmed lilies in deeper water. As the reeds spread and invade the water, this becomes clogged and marshy and, over the years, the whole pattern of plant growth moves toward the center of the pond. Of course, this does not happen in all bodies of water. People clear or harvest the reeds, and storms, flood currents, plant diseases, and hungry animals keep a natural balance.

A REED ROOF OVER THEIR HEADS
The strong, long-wearing reeds are used as roofing material in many regions, from huts in Egypt and Sudan, to houses on stilts in Indonesia and wooden cabins in southern North America. The English thatch style (above) repels rain and insulates at the same time. A skilled thatcher working with quality reeds can make a roof that remains weatherproof for 40 years or more.

CREEPING CRESS
The fool's watercress gets its name because its leaves resemble true watercress. It is found in large quantities at the back of many reed beds, and its horizontal, straggling stems add to the general tangle of vegetation.

READY FOR RECYCLING
The thick, black mud of reed-bed areas is rich in decaying plant and animal remains. Its nutrients are soon recycled by the rushes, reeds, and other plants.

Reed-bed mud

Dry land

Marshy area

Shallow water

Open water

Underground rhizome

Horizontal stems

Sweet flag

Long straight stalks

Flower head may be 8 ft (2.5 m) above the roots

Dark-greeen leaves have pale undersides

EARLY HARVEST
The reed cutter's season is usually the tail end of winter and early spring. Last year's stems are cut near the base before this year's shoots emerge, which ensures a future harvest.

THICK AND FLESHY
The juicy, strap-shaped leaves of sweet flag sprout from a thick horizontal stem. The stem has many small roots that hold the marshy mud together.

Osier shoot

The thin leaves dry very quickly when picked

Top of common reed stem

MOSES IN THE . . . ?
As a baby, Moses was supposedly hidden in a basket in a reed bed on the bank of the Nile River in Egypt. Illustrations showing this are titled *Moses in the Bulrushes* although most versions portray the baby in a clump of reed mace. This confusion has led to the name "bulrush" being given to reed mace (p. 33); the true bulrush is somewhat similar to the spike rush.

WILLOWS FOR WEAVING
Osiers are found at the back of reed beds, on less marshy ground. They have long, straight shoots and a shrubby shape. They are often coppiced (cut at ground level) to provide flexible stems ("withes") for woven chairs and baskets.

THE STRAIGHT AND NARROW
The straight, narrow stems of common reed are ideal thatching material. They are also used to make paper and other pulp-based products. Plant growth in reed beds is often very fast because there is plenty of water and nutrients, and the slender stems and leaves allow light to reach the lower levels.

Base of common reed stem

Waterside mammals

FRESHWATER HABITATS, from rivers and streams to the marshy edges of lakes and ponds, provide a home and food for a number of mammals. All the "aquatic" mammals shown here have fur coats adapted to their watery habitat. The fur of a mink, for example, is of two main types. Long, thick, flattened "guard hairs" provide physical protection and camouflaging coloration. For each guard hair there are 20 or more softer hairs of the underfur, only half as long, which trap air to keep water out and body heat in. The owners sensibly spend much time combing and cleaning their fur, keeping it in tip-top condition. Another adaptation for watery life is webs between the toes, for more efficient swimming.

FURRY FORAGER
The water shrew's dark-furred body is only about 3 in (8 cm) long. This bustling insect-eater often lives in a bankside system of narrow tunnels that press water from its coat as it squeezes through. It eats small fish, water insects, and even frogs, and hunts on dry land for worms and other small creatures.

Mink

ADAPTABLE CARNIVORE
Minks are less specialized hunters than otters and, besides fish, will eat birds, aquatic insects, and land animals such as rabbits. The broad, webbed back feet provide the main swimming power.

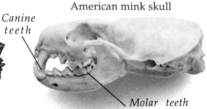

American mink skull

Canine teeth

Molar teeth

TOOTHLESS "BEAK"
When a baby platypus hatches it has teeth, but these are soon lost. Adults grind up the food of shellfish, water insects, and worms using horny plates along their jaws.

TEARERS AND CUTTERS
The mink's four long canine teeth, toward the front of its mouth, are built for catching prey and tearing flesh. The molars, at the back, are ridged for cutting.

Platypus

Platypus skull

Long bill for grinding food

DUCK'S BILL, MAMMAL'S FUR
The Australian platypus, a monotreme (egg-laying mammal), has a "bill" covered with leathery, sensitive skin. The bill is its only means of finding food - by touch - as it forages in muddy creek beds. It closes its eyes and ears when diving.

LODGE IN THE RIVER
A beaver family lives in a semi-submerged mud-and-stick house called a "lodge." The beavers build a dam of branches, twigs, stones, and mud across the stream, which raises the local water level and isolates the lodge for safety. During winter they swim under the ice to a "deep freezer" food store of woody stems and twigs.

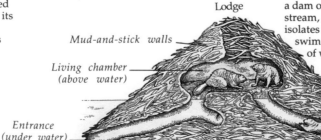

Lodge

Mud-and-stick walls

Living chamber (above water)

Food store

Raised water level

Dam

Entrance (under water)

Long canine teeth for grasping fish

Otter skull

WATCHFUL SWIMMER
Nostrils, eyes, and ears are placed high on the head so that the otter can swim almost submerged yet still breathe, look, and listen.

HUNTING THE OTTER
Otter hunting was once considered a sport and still occurs in some places, although in many countries this animal is now protected by law. Today these creatures are also at risk from pollution and from development of waterways for fishing and boating.

THE GAME OF LIFE
Otters spend much time at play, either on their own or with one another. Such "games" may help to sharpen hunting skills.

Molar teeth for grinding food

ENORMOUS GNAWERS
The beaver's large chisel-like front teeth (typical of rodents) can gnaw through tree trunks with ease.

NATURE'S LOGGERS
Beavers cut down trees for food and also to build homes in lakes they create for themselves (below left). They eat waterweeds, leaves, and other plant matter.

Beaver skull

Large incisor teeth for gnawing

FLAT SLAP
The beaver's tail is flattened and scaly. Besides its use as a rudder and paddle, it can be slapped on the water's surface to warn other beavers of danger.

Beaver

Beaver tail

Frogs, toads, and newts

AMPHIBIANS ARE ANIMALS that never quite set themselves free of the water. As their name suggests (*amphi* for "both" and *bios* for "life"), they lead a double life: in the water when young, and out of it when adult. Many adult amphibians on land must stay in damp places so that they do not dry out. This is because some species "breathe" oxygen through the skin, as well as breathing it into their lungs, and only moist skin will absorb oxygen. Young amphibians just hatched from their eggs also absorb dissolved oxygen from the water through their skin, and in addition they have gills for breathing. Some amphibians, like the common frog and toad, prefer still water in which to breed. Others, such as the hellbender, a huge salamander from North America, frequent fast-flowing water. This may be because there is more dissolved oxygen in moving water than in still water, and such large amphibians need a bigger supply. Amphibians are divided into two main groups, distinguished by their tails: newts and salamanders have them, while frogs and toads do not (except as tadpoles).

Tiger salamander

STRUNG OUT
The common toad's spawn forms a black-speckled jelly necklace, 6 ft (2 m) or more long, wrapped around plant stems.

CLUMPED TOGETHER
Common frogs lay eggs (spawn) in clumps that float below the surface. Spawn from several females may collect in one large mass.

Common frog spawn

Developing tadpole

PATCHY PATTERNING
Common frogs vary in color, but in general they are mottled with patches of olive-green and brown.

Developing tadpole

Common toad spawn

WARNING COLORATION
The vivid yellow and black blotchy pattern of the tiger salamander is thought to be a warning signal, advising potential enemies that its skin and glands produce foul-tasting liquids.

Warning coloration

Unwebbed front feet

Common toad

Cuban tree frog

Rounded fingertips bear sticky pads

One-year-old common frog

Golden lined frog

Tympanum

STICKY FINGERS
This Cuban tree frog has rounded, sticky pads on its digits, which help it grip leaves and twigs. Adults spend all their time in trees, leaving only to lay their eggs in a pond.

GOLDEN LINED FROG
A frog's "ear" (tympanum) is a disc-shaped membrane behind its eye. That frogs have good hearing is indicated by the calls and croaks they use to communicate, especially when breeding.

DRESSED IN GREEN
The startlingly green skin of Australia's dwarf tree frog hides it well among the bright leaves of its forest home.

Dwarf tree frog

GOING FOR A WALK
The squat, heavily built common toad prefers to move by walking in an unhurried fashion, though it can leap a short way when at risk. The "toes" are webbed, the "fingers" are not.

Mottled skin for camouflage

Webbed hind feet

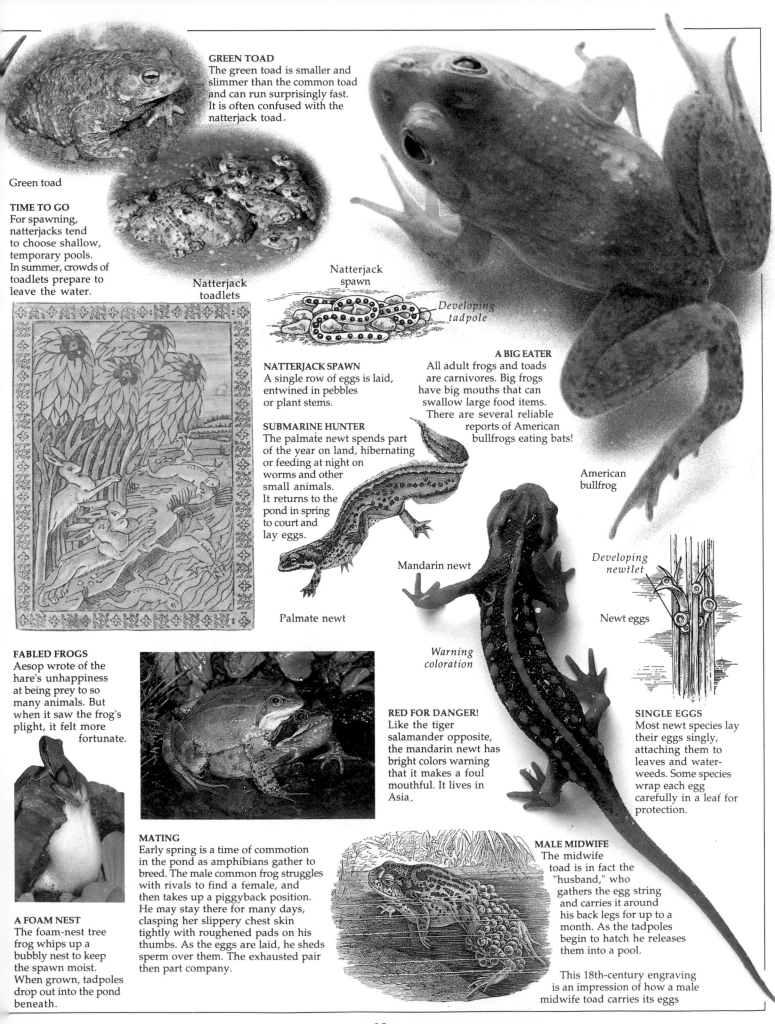

GREEN TOAD
The green toad is smaller and slimmer than the common toad and can run surprisingly fast. It is often confused with the natterjack toad.

Green toad

TIME TO GO
For spawning, natterjacks tend to choose shallow, temporary pools. In summer, crowds of toadlets prepare to leave the water.

Natterjack toadlets

Natterjack spawn

Developing tadpole

NATTERJACK SPAWN
A single row of eggs is laid, entwined in pebbles or plant stems.

SUBMARINE HUNTER
The palmate newt spends part of the year on land, hibernating or feeding at night on worms and other small animals. It returns to the pond in spring to court and lay eggs.

Palmate newt

A BIG EATER
All adult frogs and toads are carnivores. Big frogs have big mouths that can swallow large food items. There are several reliable reports of American bullfrogs eating bats!

American bullfrog

Mandarin newt

Developing newtlet

Newt eggs

Warning coloration

FABLED FROGS
Aesop wrote of the hare's unhappiness at being prey to so many animals. But when it saw the frog's plight, it felt more fortunate.

RED FOR DANGER!
Like the tiger salamander opposite, the mandarin newt has bright colors warning that it makes a foul mouthful. It lives in Asia.

SINGLE EGGS
Most newt species lay their eggs singly, attaching them to leaves and water-weeds. Some species wrap each egg carefully in a leaf for protection.

A FOAM NEST
The foam-nest tree frog whips up a bubbly nest to keep the spawn moist. When grown, tadpoles drop out into the pond beneath.

MATING
Early spring is a time of commotion in the pond as amphibians gather to breed. The male common frog struggles with rivals to find a female, and then takes up a piggyback position. He may stay there for many days, clasping her slippery chest skin tightly with roughened pads on his thumbs. As the eggs are laid, he sheds sperm over them. The exhausted pair then part company.

MALE MIDWIFE
The midwife toad is in fact the "husband," who gathers the egg string and carries it around his back legs for up to a month. As the tadpoles begin to hatch he releases them into a pool.

This 18th-century engraving is an impression of how a male midwife toad carries its eggs

Hunters in the water

MORE THAN 300 MILLION YEARS AGO, the reptiles appeared on Earth.
They probably evolved from amphibians (pp. 38-39). Their big advantage
was that they had made a complete break from life in water.
Unlike amphibians, which needed water in which to lay their
jelly-covered eggs, reptiles had hard-shelled eggs that could be
laid on land. Soon, as dinosaurs, they would come to dominate
life on land. Since that time, however, some groups of
reptiles have made an "evolutionary U-turn" and
gone back to life in the water. Many snakes readily
take to water, swim well, and hunt fish, frogs, aquatic
insects, and land creatures that come to the pond
or riverbank for a drink. Indeed, certain groups of
reptiles, such as crocodiles and turtles, have never
really left their watery environment, though they
come on to land to lay their eggs.

GIANT IN THE WATER
One of the longest, and certainly the heaviest,
of snakes is the water boa, or anaconda, of northern
South America. Lengths of 30 ft (9 m) and weights of
over 440 lb (200 kg) have been recorded. It can
consume creatures as large as a pig.

Water moccasin

Viperine water snake

DOWN IN THE SWAMPS
This old engraving shows the water moccasin,
a venomous swamp dweller of the southeastern U.S.
When this snake is threatened it opens its mouth wide
to reveal the white inside lining, hence its
other name of "cottonmouth."

*Zig zag markings on
the snake's back are
similar to those of a
common viper, or adder*

*Snake swims by
wave-like motions of its body*

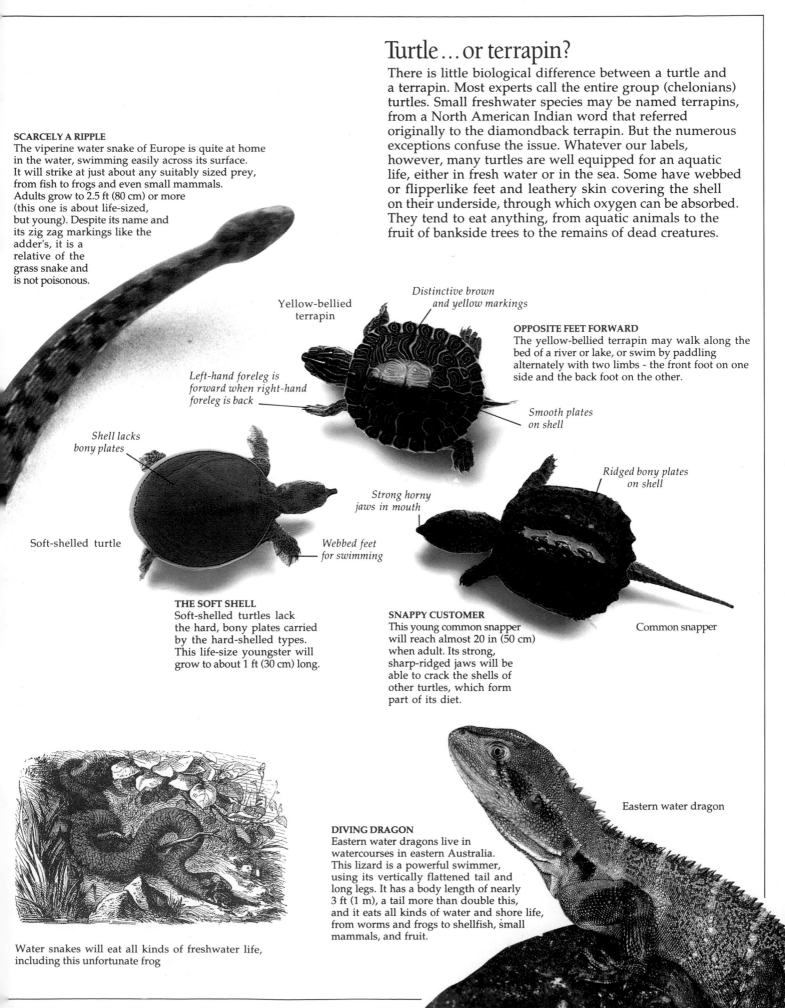

Turtle… or terrapin?

There is little biological difference between a turtle and a terrapin. Most experts call the entire group (chelonians) turtles. Small freshwater species may be named terrapins, from a North American Indian word that referred originally to the diamondback terrapin. But the numerous exceptions confuse the issue. Whatever our labels, however, many turtles are well equipped for an aquatic life, either in fresh water or in the sea. Some have webbed or flipperlike feet and leathery skin covering the shell on their underside, through which oxygen can be absorbed. They tend to eat anything, from aquatic animals to the fruit of bankside trees to the remains of dead creatures.

SCARCELY A RIPPLE
The viperine water snake of Europe is quite at home in the water, swimming easily across its surface. It will strike at just about any suitably sized prey, from fish to frogs and even small mammals. Adults grow to 2.5 ft (80 cm) or more (this one is about life-sized, but young). Despite its name and its zig zag markings like the adder's, it is a relative of the grass snake and is not poisonous.

Yellow-bellied terrapin

Distinctive brown and yellow markings

OPPOSITE FEET FORWARD
The yellow-bellied terrapin may walk along the bed of a river or lake, or swim by paddling alternately with two limbs - the front foot on one side and the back foot on the other.

Left-hand foreleg is forward when right-hand foreleg is back

Smooth plates on shell

Shell lacks bony plates

Ridged bony plates on shell

Strong horny jaws in mouth

Soft-shelled turtle

Webbed feet for swimming

THE SOFT SHELL
Soft-shelled turtles lack the hard, bony plates carried by the hard-shelled types. This life-size youngster will grow to about 1 ft (30 cm) long.

SNAPPY CUSTOMER
This young common snapper will reach almost 20 in (50 cm) when adult. Its strong, sharp-ridged jaws will be able to crack the shells of other turtles, which form part of its diet.

Common snapper

Water snakes will eat all kinds of freshwater life, including this unfortunate frog

Eastern water dragon

DIVING DRAGON
Eastern water dragons live in watercourses in eastern Australia. This lizard is a powerful swimmer, using its vertically flattened tail and long legs. It has a body length of nearly 3 ft (1 m), a tail more than double this, and it eats all kinds of water and shore life, from worms and frogs to shellfish, small mammals, and fruit.

Floating flowers

IN ANCIENT TIMES people were amazed to see that, when a previously dry watercourse filled with recent rains, the splendid blooms of water lilies would soon appear.

Flower bud

These aquatic plants gained a reputation as a symbol of immortality; the ancient Egyptians even worshipped one type of water lily, the sacred lotus. Water lily flowers are made more mysterious by their daily routine: they remain closed during the morning, open to reveal their beauty at around noon, and towards evening close again and sink slightly into the water. This may be an adaptation to aid pollination by flying insects, which are more likely to be active in the afternoon's warmth. On overcast days they might not open fully at all. During gray weather, signaling wind and rain, the closed flowers are less likely to be swamped. The flowers and leaves grow on tough, rubbery stems - 10 ft (3 m) long in some species - anchored in the mud on the beds of ponds, lakes, and slow rivers.

THE "BEAUTIFUL NUISANCE"
The water hyacinth is a free-floating flowering plant that spreads rapidly, often clogging rivers, canals, and ditches.

*Red hybrid -
"Escarboucle"*

*Leaves may be
heart shaped,
oval, or round*

*Yellow water-lily
leaves are patterned
with a red tinge.*

White water-lily flower

*Leathery leaves
repel water droplets*

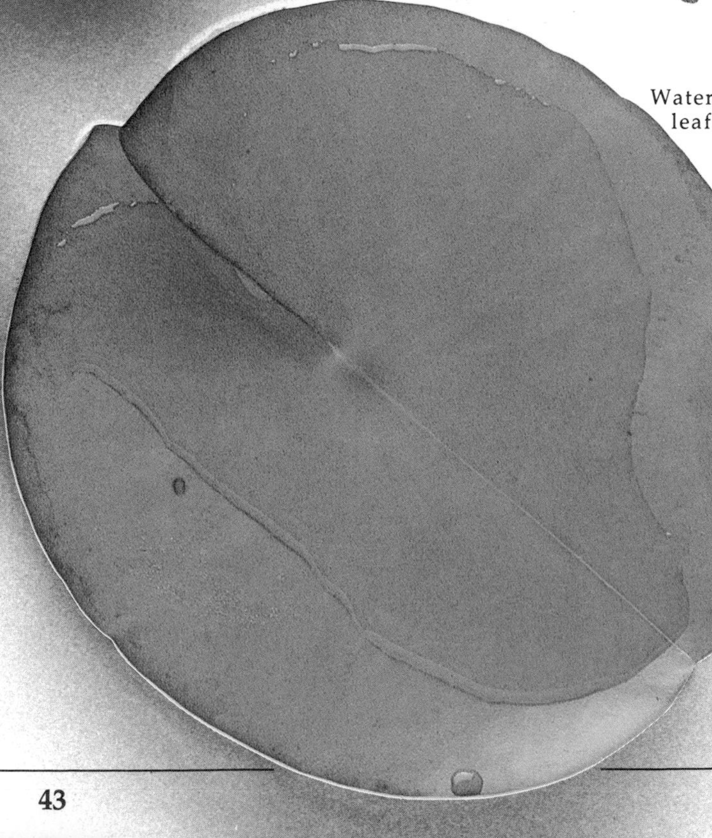

Pink hybrid

Noticeable yellow stamens

LILIES AND THEIR HYBRIDS
There are some 60 species of water lily around
the world (in some areas they are known as lotuses).
Their beautiful waxy-looking flowers and bold
circular leaves have made them favorites in ponds,
ornamental water gardens, and landscaped lakes.
Plant growers have bred many differently
colored flowers.

Yellow hybrid -
"Chromatella"

Waxy petals

Pink hybrid

FLOATING SAUCERS
Some of the largest leaves of any plant
belong to the Amazonian water lily.
A single leaf may be more than 5 ft (1.5 m)
across, with an upturned rim and stiff
reinforcing ribs beneath.

LILY LEAF CASE
The china mark moth's caterpillar cuts out
an oval of leaf and fastens it to the underside
with silk thread
to form a
protective
case.

Water-lily
leaf

WELL-USED LEAVES
The leaves (lily "pads") are used by many water creatures.
Pond snails browse on them and lay their speckled, jelly-sausage
egg masses (p. 8) on their undersides. Frogs rest on or under them,
waiting to snap up unwary insects. In some places the pads grow so
densely that certain creatures can walk on them. The African jaçana
bird has long, widespread toes and is known as the "lily trotter,"
as it steps delicately on the leaves in search of insects and seeds.

Plants at the pond's surface

MANY WATER PLANTS are not rooted in the mud at the bottom of the pond but are free to float over the surface of the water. Most have trailing roots that balance the plant and absorb minerals, and some have no roots at all. At first sight, these plants seem to have few problems. Unlike some land plants, they are well supported and, out in the middle of the pond, they cannot be shaded by trees or taller plants. But there are disadvantages: the water's surface can be whipped by the wind into waves that drag and tear at them, rain might collect on a leaf and sink it, or the leaf may be frozen under water!

SMALLEST PLANTS
The duckweeds are among the smallest and simplest flowering plants in the world. Flowers are produced only in shallow water that receives plenty of sunlight. The "leaves" contain air-filled spaces called lacunae that keep them afloat.

Tiny roots absorb minerals from the water

Blanket weed

Surface view

Side view

Duckweed

Three of the many species of duckweed are shown here

Pale-green mass is made up of hundreds of threadlike plants

New plants produced by side shoots that break off and float away

A GREEN BLANKET
"Blanket weed" is a popular name for the green hairlike masses of algae that burst into growth in the spring. These plants can spread so quickly that they cover the surface like a blanket of green wool, blocking out light to the plants below.

Two new leaves developing from old leaf

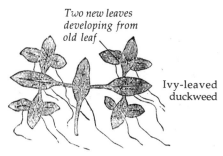

Ivy-leaved duckweed

Water lily leaf and flower bud (pp. 42-43)

FLOWERING FLOATER
This engraving shows another species of duckweed that floats on the water surface only when it is flowering; otherwise it floats just under the water surface. The ivy-leaf shape is formed when two new leaves develop, one on each side of the original leaf.

CIRCLE OF STRENGTH
Like many other floating leaves, those of water lilies have a rounded outline. This design probably helps to prevent tearing, when wind ruffles the pond surface. The shiny upper surface repels rainwater so that the leaves are not swamped by a shower. Lilies are not true floating plants because they are rooted in the mud (pp. 42-43).

Azolla water fern

Pink tinge develops to deep red in autumn

Threadlike roots trail beneath the plant

FLOATING FRONDS
Azolla is not a flowering plant but a fern, so technically its delicately sculptured "leaves" are called fronds. Tiny hairs repel water and keep the fronds from becoming waterlogged and sinking.

Leaves are similar in shape to water lily leaves

WINTER SEEDS AND BUDS
Frogbit, a relative of water soldier (below), has a similar way of avoiding the ice and frost of winter. In this case, however, the parts that survive the winter are the seeds and the specially grown, dense "winter buds." Both are produced in the autumn and sink to rest in the mud, until the increasing light levels and temperatures of spring spur them into growth, when they float to the surface again. In summer, the delicate white flowers and kidney-shaped leaves carpet whole ponds and ditches.

Frogbit

Plants will sometimes root in shallow water

Water soldier

Trailing roots

GREEN ROSETTES
The rosettes of water soldier spend summer floating at or near the pond surface. As autumn approaches, the leaves develop a limy coating that weighs them down. The plant sinks, avoiding winter's frost and ice. Fresh spring leaves lift it up again. This plant reproduces by sending out runners that root at a distance, and by male and female flowers borne on separate plants.

WATER SOLDIER IN FLOWER
White flowers are produced in midsummer, with male and female flowers on different plants. Once flowering is over, the plant sinks to the bottom of the pond.

Long, unbranched roots hang down under the plant to balance it

Underwater weeds

Sᴜʙᴍᴇʀɢᴇᴅ ᴡᴇᴇᴅs ɢʀᴏᴡ ɪɴ ᴘᴏɴᴅs ᴀɴᴅ ʀɪᴠᴇʀs like trees in a miniature underwater forest. They provide shelter for some animals, and places of ambush for others which dash and grab unwary victims swimming by. The weeds are food for many creatures, from pond snails to ducks. They also provide that most vital substance, oxygen. As a plant carries out photosynthesis, capturing the sun's light energy to build new tissues, it produces oxygen as a by-product. The oxygen filters into the water and is used by both plants and animals for the process of respiration. On a sunny day, small bubbles of oxygen can be seen coating underwater plants and occasionally rising to the surface.

Rigid hornwort

CURTAIN OF ROOTS
The water violet's abundant roots hang like a veil in the water. The stem grows out of the water, where it bears not leaves but pale, pinkish five-petaled flowers.

Water violet

TOTAL SUBMERSION
Feathery-looking hornworts are completely at home in the water. Even the flowers are submerged, growing where the leaf joins the stem.

New Zealand pygmyweed

GREEN BALL
Volvox is a microscopic water plant and an important food for tiny creatures.

Trailing roots

Canadian waterweed

NEW ZEALAND PYGMYWEED
This plant is causing concern in many waterways because of its uncontrolled spread. It was first introduced to bring oxygen into the water.

ACROSS THE ATLANTIC
Canadian waterweed left its North American home in about 1840, soon colonizing and clogging up European ponds and rivers.

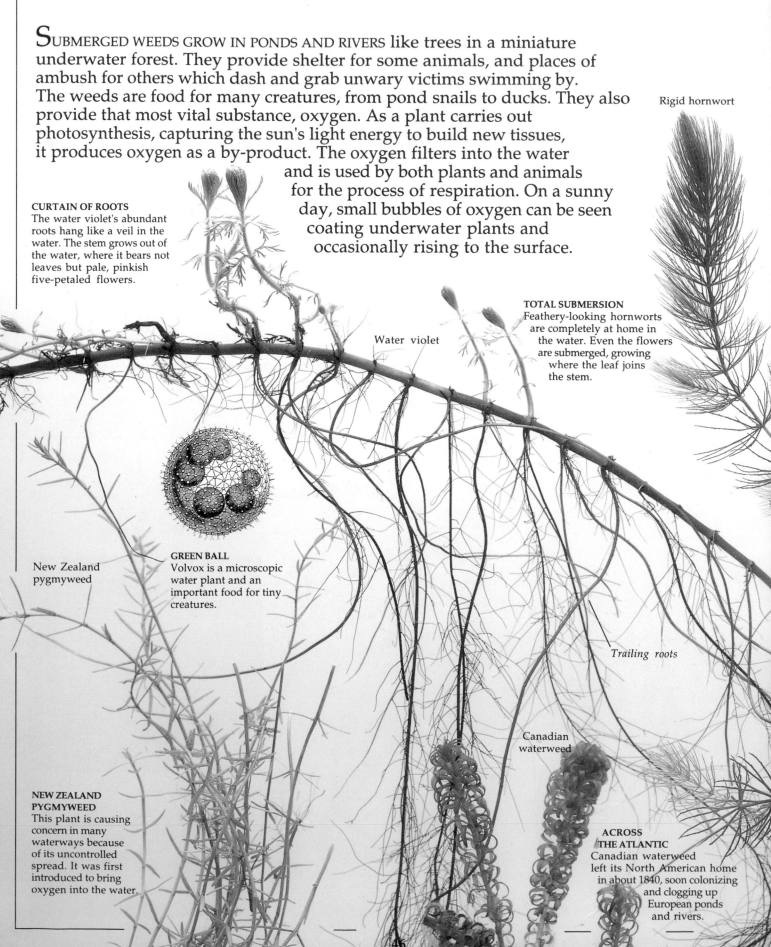

POND "PLANKTON"
At 25X magnification, the microscopic world of underwater plants is revealed.

PERCH IN THE GRASS
Tape grass is one of the popularly named "river" grasses. It offers a hideout for fish, particularly the perch, which is camouflaged by its vertical stripes (p. 23).

Tape grass

Bulbous rush

Narrow leaves resemble the needles of a fir tree

SLENDER WATERWEED
The pale-green water starwort sways in clumps in the water.

FLUSHED RUSH
The bulbous rush is usually rooted on the pond's side, but sometimes it grows underwater, and becomes very long.

Water starwort

47

Dragonflies and damselflies

THESE LARGE, POWERFUL FLYERS speed back and forth along the bank and over the water's surface, using their enormous eyes to search out small creatures. Like those of other insects, the dragonfly's eyes are made up of many separate lenses that probably give a mosaic-like picture of the world. As the adults dart about above, the water-dwelling nymphs (babies) crawl on the pond bottom. Like their parents, they seize and eat any small creature they can catch, from other water insects to tadpoles and fish.

Cast-off nymphal skin

Broad-bodied libellula nymph

Young southern hawker nymph

Mask — Hooks on mask spear prey — Mask

THE DEADLY MASK
Dragonfly nymphs are the scourge of the pond, eating anything they can catch with their "mask." This is a horny flap, like the lower lip, which has two vicious hooks at the end (above). Normally the mask is folded under the head, but it is hinged so that it can suddenly shoot out to spear prey, which is then pulled back to the mouth.

Damselflies

These are smaller and more slender relatives of dragonflies. Although at first glance they appear very similar in shape and way of life, there are several important differences that set them apart from the dragonflies - most obviously the fact that the damselfly holds its two pairs of wings together over its back when resting, while the dragonfly holds them out flat at the sides of its body.

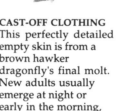

CAST-OFF CLOTHING
This perfectly detailed empty skin is from a brown hawker dragonfly's final molt. New adults usually emerge at night or early in the morning, to avoid enemies.

THE MATING GAME
The male dragonfly clasps the female and she bends to pick up the sperm from a special organ at the front of his abdomen.

SIMILAR WINGS
A damselfly's wings are roughly equal in size, with rounded ends, unlike the dragonfly's wings.

Blue-tailed damselfly

Emerald damselfly

Eyes protrude from side of head

Rounded wing tips

MALE AND FEMALE
In most damselflies, the female has a slightly wider and less colorful abdomen than the male.

Azure damselfly

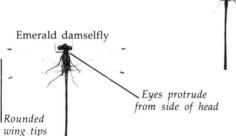

Large red damselfly

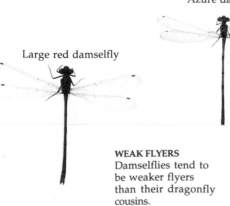

SMALLER EYES
The small eyes of the damselfly are set on the sides of the head; the dragonfly's eyes meet at the top of the head.

WEAK FLYERS
Damselflies tend to be weaker flyers than their dragonfly cousins.

THE LIFE OF THE DRAGONFLY
A dragonfly begins life as an egg laid in water. It hatches into a larva that grows by splitting its skin and forming a new, larger skin. There are between eight and 15 molts over two years or more, depending on the species. A gradual change to adult form like this (compared with a sudden change; for example, caterpillar to butterfly) is called "incomplete metamorphosis." During the in-between stages the insect is referred to as a nymph. Finally the nymph climbs up a stem into the air, splits its skin a final time, and the adult emerges.

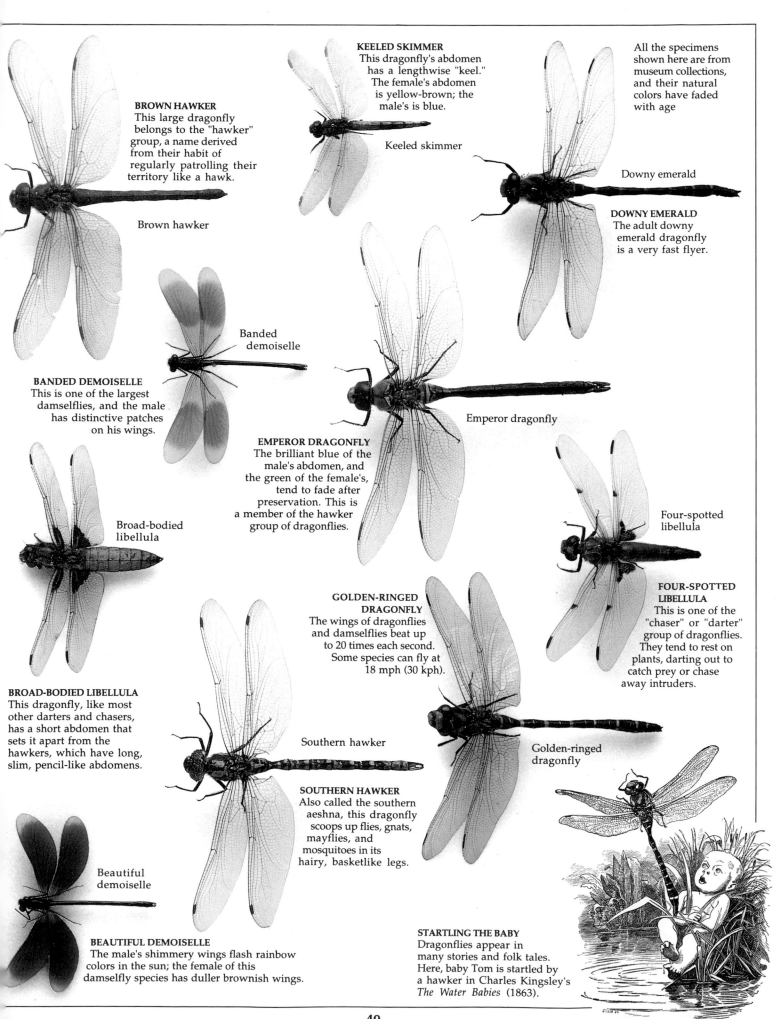

BROWN HAWKER
This large dragonfly belongs to the "hawker" group, a name derived from their habit of regularly patrolling their territory like a hawk.

Brown hawker

KEELED SKIMMER
This dragonfly's abdomen has a lengthwise "keel." The female's abdomen is yellow-brown; the male's is blue.

Keeled skimmer

All the specimens shown here are from museum collections, and their natural colors have faded with age

Downy emerald

DOWNY EMERALD
The adult downy emerald dragonfly is a very fast flyer.

Banded demoiselle

BANDED DEMOISELLE
This is one of the largest damselflies, and the male has distinctive patches on his wings.

Broad-bodied libellula

Emperor dragonfly

EMPEROR DRAGONFLY
The brilliant blue of the male's abdomen, and the green of the female's, tend to fade after preservation. This is a member of the hawker group of dragonflies.

Four-spotted libellula

FOUR-SPOTTED LIBELLULA
This is one of the "chaser" or "darter" group of dragonflies. They tend to rest on plants, darting out to catch prey or chase away intruders.

BROAD-BODIED LIBELLULA
This dragonfly, like most other darters and chasers, has a short abdomen that sets it apart from the hawkers, which have long, slim, pencil-like abdomens.

GOLDEN-RINGED DRAGONFLY
The wings of dragonflies and damselflies beat up to 20 times each second. Some species can fly at 18 mph (30 kph).

Southern hawker

Golden-ringed dragonfly

SOUTHERN HAWKER
Also called the southern aeshna, this dragonfly scoops up flies, gnats, mayflies, and mosquitoes in its hairy, basketlike legs.

Beautiful demoiselle

BEAUTIFUL DEMOISELLE
The male's shimmery wings flash rainbow colors in the sun; the female of this damselfly species has duller brownish wings.

STARTLING THE BABY
Dragonflies appear in many stories and folk tales. Here, baby Tom is startled by a hawker in Charles Kingsley's *The Water Babies* (1863).

49

Insects in the water

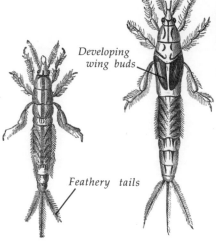

Developing wing buds

Feathery tails

Iɴsᴇᴄᴛs, the most adaptable creatures on earth, can live in places ranging from glaciers to hot springs, from deserts to tropical forests. About half of the 25 major groups of insects live in fresh water. Some, such as water beetles and bugs, spend nearly all their lives in water. Others, like mayflies and caddis flies, have a watery "childhood" and emerge into the air when adult. Certain aquatic insects, including the water beetles, are air-breathing and visit the surface regularly to obtain supplies, which they store by various clever means (p. 51). Others have specialized "gills" to take oxygen from the water, and still others can absorb dissolved oxygen through their skin.

Like dragonfly larvae (p. 48), mayfly larvae are called nymphs

As the nymph matures, small "wing buds" grow with each molt

Rat-tailed maggots (drone fly larvae)

Breathing tube

Adult drone fly

MAGGOT'S PARENT
The rat-tailed maggot is the larva of the drone fly, a type of hover fly, named because it looks like the drones of the honey bee.

Adult mayfly

Long "tails" identify this insect

MAGGOT WITH SNORKEL *above*
The rat-tailed maggot has a long breathing tube of three sections that telescope into one another. It lives in the mud of shallow ponds, sucking up decaying food.

THREE-TAILED FLY
Like its larvae, the adult mayfly has three very distinctive trailing "tails." Mayflies are known as "spinners" by people who fish.

GROWN-UP CADDIS
Adult caddis flies are less well-known than their water-dwelling youngsters. The adults are drab gray or brown, come out at dusk or night, and are easily confused with small moths. They flit about near water, rarely feed, and seldom live more than a few days.

SPRING FEAST
Mayfly adults emerge in huge swarms in spring. They fly weakly, have no mouths and so cannot feed, and spend their few days of adult life mating and laying eggs by dipping their abdomens in water. The "dance of the mayflies" attracts hungry fish - and anglers (people who fish) who use mayfly lures to catch trout.

Adult caddis flies

Wings covered with fine hairs

Antennae often as long as the body

STICKS AND STONES
Many species of caddis fly have aquatic larvae that build protective cases around themselves. The construction material is characteristic of each species. As the larva grows, it adds more material to the front of the case.

Larval cases may be attached to water plants or lie on the pond bottom

Plant stalks

Small stones

Discarded snail shells

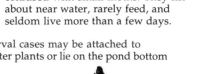

Case is extended by adding material to the front end

Head of larva emerges from case to feed

Every species makes a distinctive case

Entrance to case

Cases built by caddisfly larvae

Front legs seize prey   Water stick insect

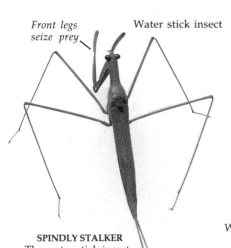

SPINDLY STALKER
The water stick insect grabs any small underwater creature with its mantis-like front legs and then sucks the juices from inside, using its needle-shaped mouthparts. A short trip to the surface allows fresh supplies of air to be sucked through the long tail, the two parts of which are usually held together by bristles to form a tube.

Parts of breathing tube

Front legs catch tadpoles and other prey

Water scorpion

Breathing tube

STING IN THE TAIL?
No, the "tail" of the water scorpion is a harmless breathing tube, unlike the poisonous version of its dry-land namesake. The dangerous parts are the powerful clawlike front legs and stinging beak-shaped mouth.

Water scorpion

DEAD LEAF?
When disturbed, the water scorpion sinks to the bottom and stays still, looking like a dead leaf.

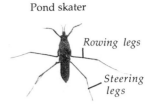

Pond skater

Rowing legs

Steering legs

WATER WALKER
The back four feet of the pond skater have thick pads of hair that repel water, and keep this bug from sinking as it rows across the surface of the pond.

Wing covers

Back swimmer

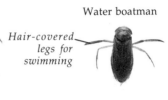

BACK SWIMMER . . .
The back swimmer is a bug, not a beetle. This unusual top view shows its hard wing cases that cover strong flying wings. Most of its time, however, is spent hanging upside down below the water surface.

Water boatman

Hair-covered legs for swimming

WATER BOATMAN
This insect's name refers to the oarlike rowing motions of its legs as it moves itself through the water. It eats any plant debris or algae it can grub up or catch in its sieve-like front legs.

Air bubble

THE BUBBLE CHAMBER
The air-breathing water spider (not actually an insect but an arachnid) makes a "diving bell" to live in. It weaves a web among water plants and stocks it with air from the surface (below). The air being transported in its body hairs gives the spider's abdomen a silvery sheen (left).

BEETLE POWER
In a small pond, the great diving beetle has few predators but many prey - insects, tadpoles, and small fish such as this unlucky stickleback.

SPARE AIR
Water beetles are air-breathing insects and have devised clever methods for collecting air from the surface. Many aquatic beetles trap air on the hairs under their bodies. Others trap air under their wing cases, making them buoyant and always struggling to swim downward. Some, like the silver water beetle shown here, use both methods.

Silver water beetle

Freshwater shells

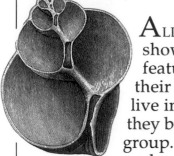

ALL THE LIFE-SIZED SHELLS shown here have two features in common: their builder-owners live in fresh water, and they belong to the mollusk group. The mollusk's shell is made chiefly of calcium-containing minerals such as calcium carbonate (lime). To make its shell, the animal must absorb minerals from the water. In general, aquatic mollusks are more common in "hard-water" areas, where water is naturally richer in dissolved minerals. The mussels and cockles (bivalves) feed by sucking in a stream of water and filtering out tiny food particles. Most snails and limpets (gastropods) "graze", on water plants and the algal "scum" on submerged stones, but some species can filter-feed.

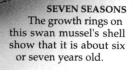

SEVEN SEASONS
The growth rings on this swan mussel's shell show that it is about six or seven years old.

How do mollusks breathe?

Water snails are divided into two groups, depending on how they breathe. The great pond snail, ram's-horn snail, and bladder snail are known as pulmonates - they breathe air, like land snails. They float up to the surface, open a breathing aperture (hole) and take a gulp of air into a lung-like cavity. The other group, including valve, river, and spire snails, are called prosobranchs. They breathe by absorbing oxygen from the water through gills.

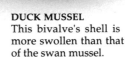

DUCK MUSSEL
This bivalve's shell is more swollen than that of the swan mussel.

RIGHT-HANDERS
Usually great pond snail shells curl to the right, but "left-handers" are known.

SEE-THROUGH SNAIL
The nautilus ram's-horn is so small that its shell is semi-transparent.

BIVALVE LARDER
Pea mussels are the staple food of many fish and water birds.

WANDERING SNAIL
The whorls of this wandering snail are squashed up at its tip.

CURLY WHORLY
The tightly coiled white ram's-horn is from ponds and streams.

MARBLED SNAIL
The nerite snail has an attractively speckled and whorled shell.

JOINTED SHELL
The horny pea cockle is a bivalve mollusk as it has two shells.

River shellfish

The mollusks below and left (swan and duck mussels) tend to live in flowing water, rather than the still waters of ponds and lakes. The growth rings of the mussels indicate their age, which might be up to a dozen years for a large individual. Growth rings can be seen on snails, too, but they are less clearly divided into a year-by-year pattern.

Snails grow by adding new material at the open end of the shell

TWISTING TUBE
Snail shells are coiled, gradually widening tubes, clearly seen on this Lister's river snail.

MINERAL COLLECTOR
River snail's shells may be over 2 in (5 cm) long - a lot of calcium to collect.

LISTENING SNAIL
The ear pond snail's flared opening resembles a human ear.

SWOLLEN JOINT
This tumid unio mussel has an inflated "umbo" near its hinge line.

ZEBRA MUSSEL
This bivalve is anchored to rocks by sticky threads.

WATERWEED EATER
The great ram's-horn water snail browses on underwater plants.

DISTINCTIVE SHELL
The last whorl on the bladder snail's shell is very large.

STUBBY AND SHINY
These shiny, compact shells belong to the common bithynia.

BITHYNIA LEACHI
These bithynias have no common name; only a scientific name.

STRAIGHT SNAIL
The river limpet is a true snail, but its shell is not coiled.

OPEN AND SHUT
The "valve" of the valve snail is the door or operculum, of its shell.

SLOW WATER
The lake limpet can often be found in slow-flowing rivers.

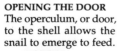

OPENING THE DOOR
The operculum, or door, to the shell allows the snail to emerge to feed.

Operculum makes a watertight seal to shell when closed

TWO TINY SHELLS
Pea shell cockles are tiny, filter-feeding bivalve mollusks.

SALTY AND FRESH
Jenkin's spire shells are found in estuaries as well as in ponds and rivers.

The head of the river

MANY RIVERS begin life as fast-flowing upland streams, cascading across open areas or through craggy woodlands. The deep, rocky gulleys, the overhanging trees, and the splashing waters create contrasting worlds: damp, shady banks with lush green vegetation, and stream beds where rushing water washes away nearly all plant life and any but the most stubbornly clinging animals. In a flood, entire plant and animal communities may be swept away. Yet somehow new seeds and spores soon spring up, and creatures creep out from under rocks to fight their way back upstream.

Dipper

UNDERWATER WALKER
The dipper bobs its head as it stands on midstream rocks, watching for small animal prey. It can also walk along the river-bed, head facing upstream and tail acting as a rudder in the current, to keep its feet firmly on the bottom.

ARMORED CRAYFISH
Hard (mineral-rich) water is favored by the freshwater crayfish, a relative of the marine lobster. It needs plenty of calcium minerals to build its shell.

BANKSIDE MOISTURE LOVERS
Succulent growths of mosses, liverworts, ferns, and other damp-loving plants colonize the banks and splash-zone rocks. The larger heart-shaped leaves are marsh violet.

Hard outer shell made up from minerals in the water

Freshwater crayfish

Polytrichum moss

Fern

Puffball

Liverwort

YOUNG BALL
Fungi, such as this young member of the puffball group, prefer shady stream-side conditions.

LICHEN BRANCH
Shady, damp conditions are ideal for certain lichens, which are co-operative combinations of fungi and algae. Two different kinds of leafy lichen are growing on this branch.

Great wood rush

Liverwort

Marsh violet

Bullhead

UPSTREAM FISH
Despite the fast current fish, such as the bullhead, are found at the head of the river. The bullhead's flattened shape allows it to hide under stones.

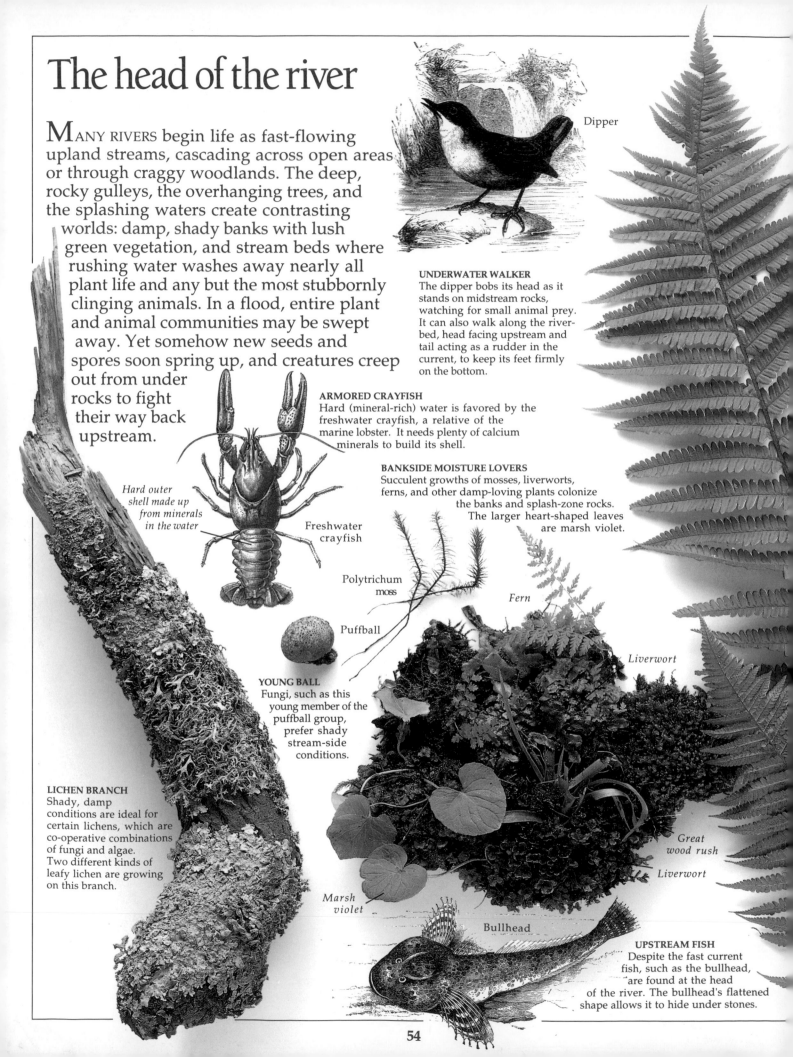

Oak leaves

FOOD FROM ABOVE
Trees such as the oak hang over the water, and if their fruits and leaves fall into the water they provide food for river-dwellers.

Fontinalis moss

Acorns

Galls (swellings) caused by insects

Deeply divided fronds

Great wood rush

BETWEEN THE BOULDERS
Groups of midstream boulders often support a thriving island of life; here, great wood rush sprouts from soil collected by the current.

UNDERWATER MOSS
Fontinalis or "willow moss," anchored to a stone or fallen log, moves back and forth with the current in slower streams and rivers.

Shiny, undivided fronds

Rows of spores

Male fern

Layer of moss growing on boulders

FEATHERY FRONDS
Many types of ferns thrive in the shaded, humid conditions along riverbanks. The hart's-tongue fern (far right) has riblike rows of brown spore cases on the undersides of its fronds. It is unusual among ferns in having solid, unbranched fronds.

Feathery, pale-green fronds

Shiny, dark-green fronds

Hard-fern

Lady fern

Hart's-tongue fern

Brown spore cases

Life along the riverbank

As STREAMS BECOME MORE SEDATE and their courses join up and widen, the river comes into being. But when does a stream become a river? One definition is that streams are less than 15 ft (5 m) wide, while rivers are more. Larger rivers usually have a slower current, allowing rooted plants to grow well at the water's edge. Whatever the distinction, riverbank life suits many kinds of plants and animals. On a high-banked river, the soil at the water's edge is nearly always saturated, but it becomes drier higher up the bank. So plant life often grows in zones, with mud-rooted irises and water plantains lower down, and the damp-ground hemp agrimony, balsam, and similar flowers slightly higher.

Thistle-shaped flower head

ABOUT TO FLOWER
This teasel's flower is just coming out, its pinkish-mauve petals not yet visible.

FIVE IN ONE
Each small "flower" of hemp agrimony is a cluster of five even smaller "florets."

Hooks attach fruits to passing animals

Teasel

Spiny flower head is still developing

Heart-shaped leaves are slightly downy

Exploring along the river has long been a favorite leisure pastime

Explosive seedcases are developing inside the flowers

Hemp agrimony

Leaves have toothed edges

HITCHING A RIDE
Young great burdock flowers already bear the hooks that, when the seeds ripen, will catch on fur, coats, and socks.

TRAVELING FLOWER
Indian, or Himalayan, balsam, a native of that region, has spread along many riverbanks, ditch sides and damp gulleys.

Leaves have serrated margins

Stem has reddish tinge

Indian balsam
(Himalayan balsam)

HIGH-WATER MARK
The river's spring flood left surface debris stuck to this overhanging twig, 3 ft (1 m) above summer's water level.

Old plant stalks caught around twig

The pyramid-shaped blossoms make water plantain a dramatic plant on the riverbank.

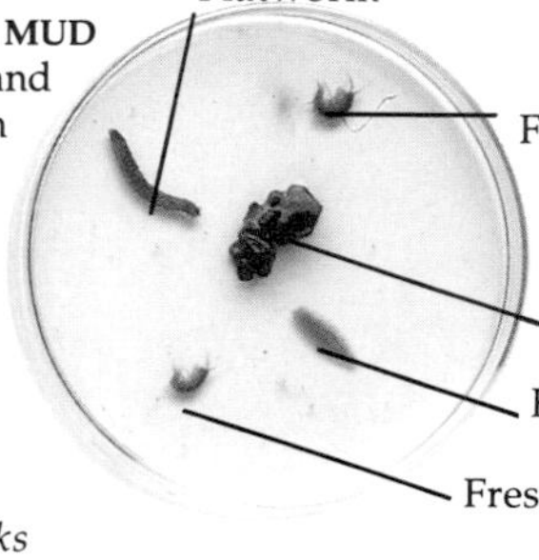

Water plantain leaf

Water plantain blossoms

RIVERBANK HOME
Many mammals use the riverbank as a home. Otters live in well-hidden "holts" in the bank vegetation or under overhanging tree roots.

Flatworm

DOWN IN THE MUD
The beds of ponds and rivers abound with small animals such as these, which are food for fish and other creatures.

Freshwater shrimp

The caddis larva has built its case from tiny pebbles (p. 50)

Flatworm

Freshwater shrimp

Toothmarks of mammal

Loaches

BARBEL-BEARD
The barbels, or "whiskers," of the loach are used as feeling organs. This river dweller emerges from under stones after dusk to hunt in the mud for worms, insects, and other small water life.

Water starwort provides cover for these shy fish

AFTERNOON OPENING
Water plantain roots in the mud at the edges of small rivers. Its flowers are closed for most of the morning and evening, and open only after noon.

Tiny lilac flowers

Tiny mollusks attached to stone

Yellow flag leaves

ANONYMOUS NIBBLER
These yellow flag leaves from a steep riverbank have been nibbled by a hungry mammal.

CLAMPING DOWN
Under their rounded shells, the "feet" of these tiny freshwater mollusks grasp this rock firmly.

The river's mouth

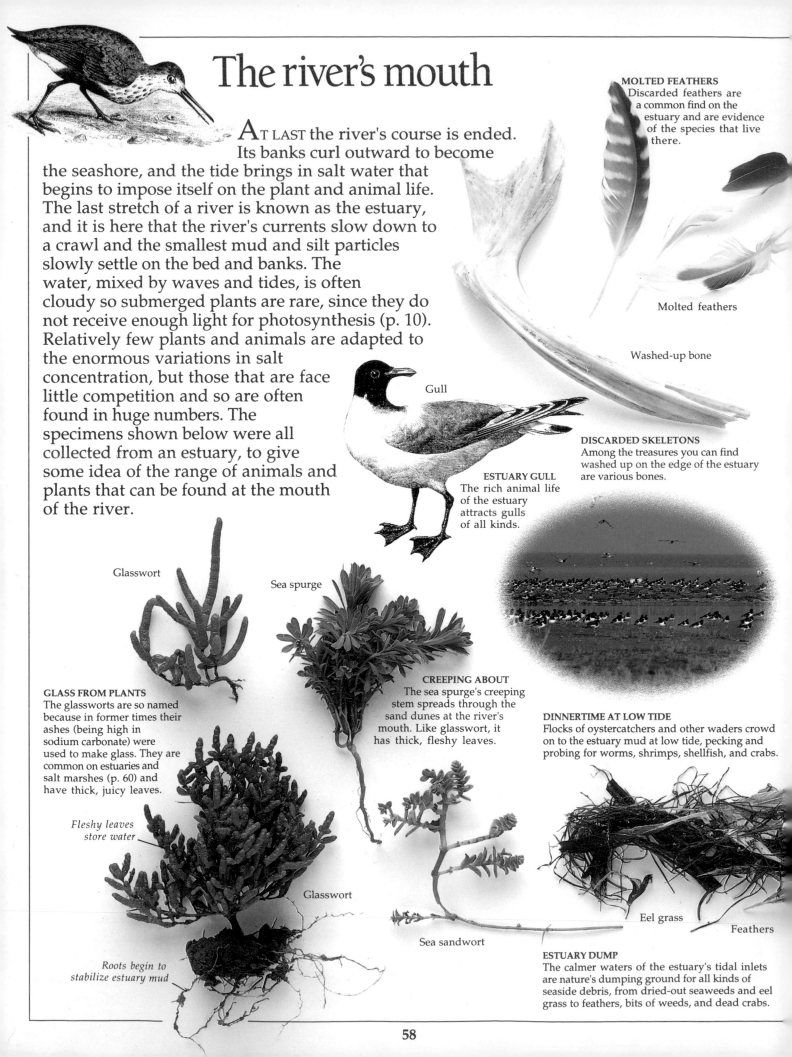

AT LAST the river's course is ended. Its banks curl outward to become the seashore, and the tide brings in salt water that begins to impose itself on the plant and animal life. The last stretch of a river is known as the estuary, and it is here that the river's currents slow down to a crawl and the smallest mud and silt particles slowly settle on the bed and banks. The water, mixed by waves and tides, is often cloudy so submerged plants are rare, since they do not receive enough light for photosynthesis (p. 10). Relatively few plants and animals are adapted to the enormous variations in salt concentration, but those that are face little competition and so are often found in huge numbers. The specimens shown below were all collected from an estuary, to give some idea of the range of animals and plants that can be found at the mouth of the river.

MOLTED FEATHERS
Discarded feathers are a common find on the estuary and are evidence of the species that live there.

Molted feathers

Washed-up bone

Gull

ESTUARY GULL
The rich animal life of the estuary attracts gulls of all kinds.

DISCARDED SKELETONS
Among the treasures you can find washed up on the edge of the estuary are various bones.

Glasswort

Sea spurge

GLASS FROM PLANTS
The glassworts are so named because in former times their ashes (being high in sodium carbonate) were used to make glass. They are common on estuaries and salt marshes (p. 60) and have thick, juicy leaves.

CREEPING ABOUT
The sea spurge's creeping stem spreads through the sand dunes at the river's mouth. Like glasswort, it has thick, fleshy leaves.

DINNERTIME AT LOW TIDE
Flocks of oystercatchers and other waders crowd on to the estuary mud at low tide, pecking and probing for worms, shrimps, shellfish, and crabs.

Fleshy leaves store water

Glasswort

Sea sandwort

Eel grass

Feathers

Roots begin to stabilize estuary mud

ESTUARY DUMP
The calmer waters of the estuary's tidal inlets are nature's dumping ground for all kinds of seaside debris, from dried-out seaweeds and eel grass to feathers, bits of weeds, and dead crabs.

A LOT TO LEARN
Oystercatcher chicks hatch from eggs laid in open or short vegetation around the estuary. The chicks can take up to 26 weeks to learn the specialized feeding techniques from their parents.

Winkles

Tellina

Cockle

Periwinkle

Mussel

Young crab

Oyster shell

Tellina shell

Cockleshell

Hole pecked by bird

Cockleshell

Tellina shell

HOLE IN ONE
These mollusk shells have been pecked through by estuary birds and the animal inside has been eaten.

Oystercatcher and chick

UNDER THE BREAKWATER
Any "obstruction" on the flat estuary, such as a breakwater or pier, soon becomes colonized by a variety of life that can tolerate the different salt levels. The sea slater is a crustacean, cousin of the wood louse, and also a relative of the crab.

Sea slater

Lugworm

Oyster shell

SHORE WORM
Squiggly marks on the estuary mud mark the position of a lugworm's U-shaped burrow.

Sheldrake and chick

Barnacles

Slipper limpet

Cockle-shell

SHELDRAKE DUCKLING
Young sheldrakes look like most other ducklings, but the adults look more like geese. This waterfowl eats not only shellfish but also fish, worms, and other small animals.

Razor shell

IN FROM THE SEA
The shells of true seashore mollusks are often washed up on the estuary shore, as was this small barnacle-encrusted stone, loosened by a storm.

Crab

PIPEFISH
This relative of the seahorse has hardened outer skin and moves using its dorsal (back) fin. It copes well in the changing salt levels of estuary water.

Pipefish

Spiral wrack

SHORE WEED
In the more sheltered and seaward sites, shore algae can gain a foothold. This spiral wrack is characteristic of the upper shore zone.

The salt marsh

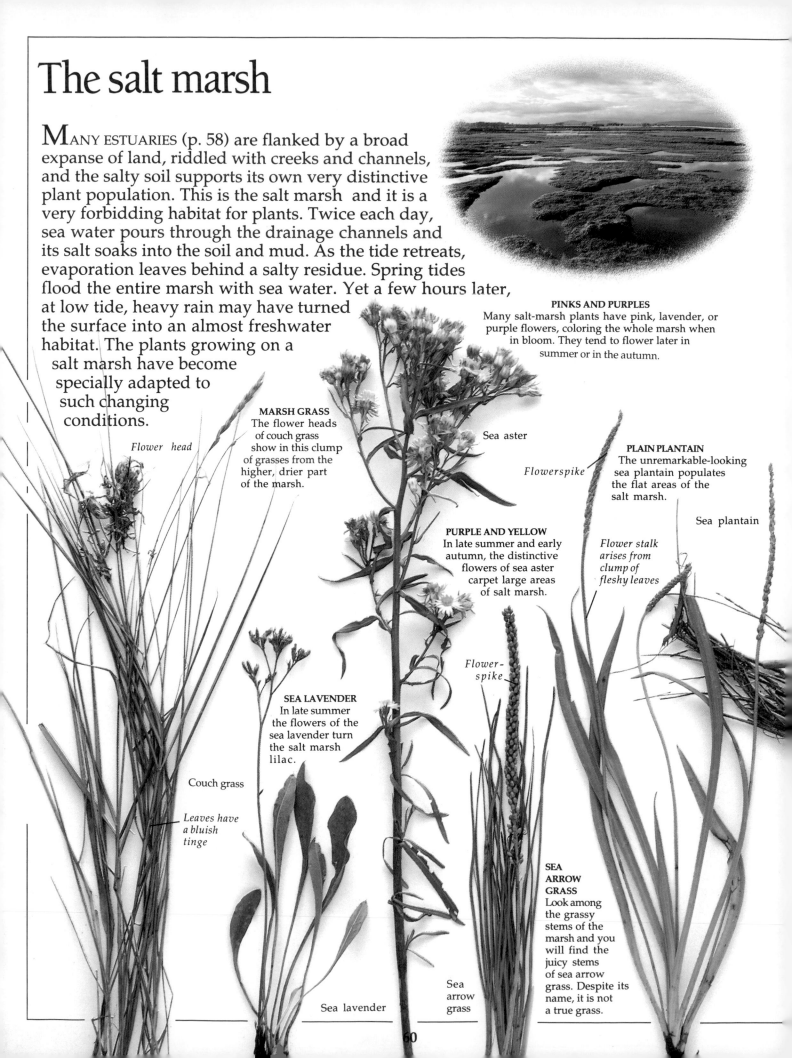

MANY ESTUARIES (p. 58) are flanked by a broad expanse of land, riddled with creeks and channels, and the salty soil supports its own very distinctive plant population. This is the salt marsh and it is a very forbidding habitat for plants. Twice each day, sea water pours through the drainage channels and its salt soaks into the soil and mud. As the tide retreats, evaporation leaves behind a salty residue. Spring tides flood the entire marsh with sea water. Yet a few hours later, at low tide, heavy rain may have turned the surface into an almost freshwater habitat. The plants growing on a salt marsh have become specially adapted to such changing conditions.

PINKS AND PURPLES
Many salt-marsh plants have pink, lavender, or purple flowers, coloring the whole marsh when in bloom. They tend to flower later in summer or in the autumn.

Flower head

MARSH GRASS
The flower heads of couch grass show in this clump of grasses from the higher, drier part of the marsh.

Sea aster

Flowerspike

PLAIN PLANTAIN
The unremarkable-looking sea plantain populates the flat areas of the salt marsh.

Sea plantain

PURPLE AND YELLOW
In late summer and early autumn, the distinctive flowers of sea aster carpet large areas of salt marsh.

Flower stalk arises from clump of fleshy leaves

SEA LAVENDER
In late summer the flowers of the sea lavender turn the salt marsh lilac.

Flower-spike

Couch grass

Leaves have a bluish tinge

SEA ARROW GRASS
Look among the grassy stems of the marsh and you will find the juicy stems of sea arrow grass. Despite its name, it is not a true grass.

Sea lavender

Sea arrow grass

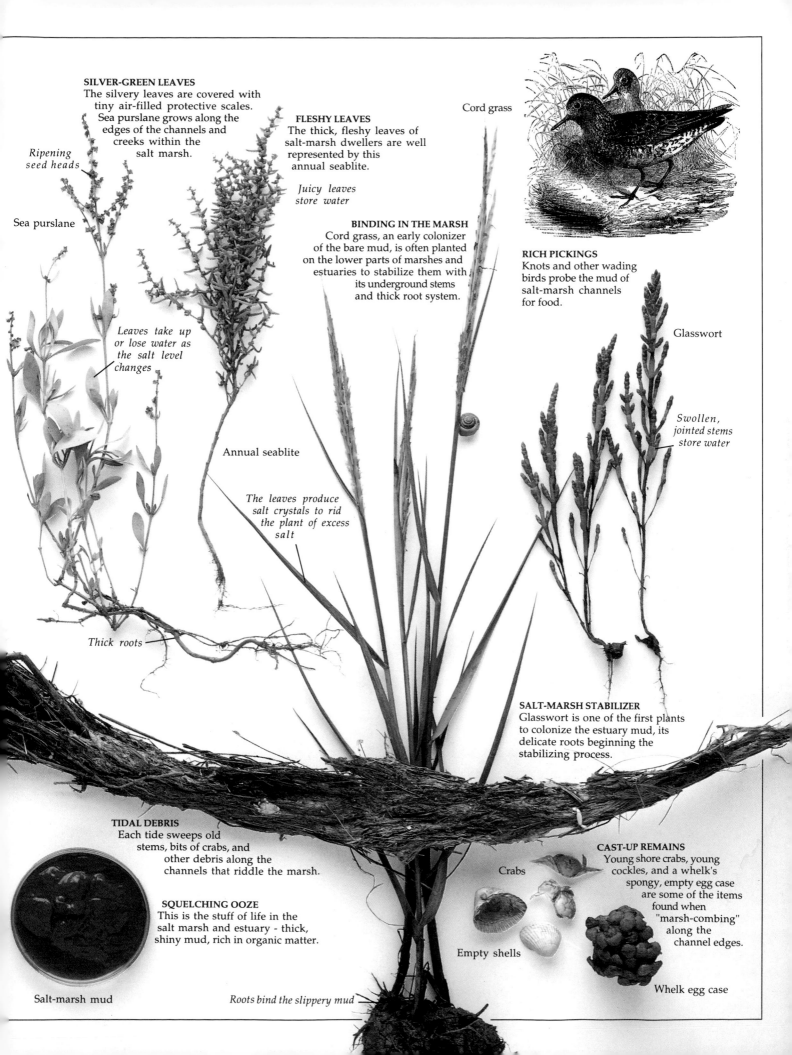

SILVER-GREEN LEAVES
The silvery leaves are covered with
tiny air-filled protective scales.
Sea purslane grows along the
edges of the channels and
creeks within the
salt marsh.

*Ripening
seed heads*

Sea purslane

*Leaves take up
or lose water as
the salt level
changes*

FLESHY LEAVES
The thick, fleshy leaves of
salt-marsh dwellers are well
represented by this
annual seablite.

*Juicy leaves
store water*

BINDING IN THE MARSH
Cord grass, an early colonizer
of the bare mud, is often planted
on the lower parts of marshes and
estuaries to stabilize them with
its underground stems
and thick root system.

Cord grass

RICH PICKINGS
Knots and other wading
birds probe the mud of
salt-marsh channels
for food.

Glasswort

*Swollen,
jointed stems
store water*

Annual seablite

*The leaves produce
salt crystals to rid
the plant of excess
salt*

Thick roots

SALT-MARSH STABILIZER
Glasswort is one of the first plants
to colonize the estuary mud, its
delicate roots beginning the
stabilizing process.

TIDAL DEBRIS
Each tide sweeps old
stems, bits of crabs, and
other debris along the
channels that riddle the marsh.

SQUELCHING OOZE
This is the stuff of life in the
salt marsh and estuary - thick,
shiny mud, rich in organic matter.

Crabs

CAST-UP REMAINS
Young shore crabs, young
cockles, and a whelk's
spongy, empty egg case
are some of the items
found when
"marsh-combing"
along the
channel edges.

Empty shells

Whelk egg case

Salt-marsh mud

Roots bind the slippery mud

Study and conservation

THE FASCINATING WILDLIFE OF PONDS AND RIVERS is suffering in our modern world. Pollution, the demand for housing and farm land, and more people using the water for relaxation and recreation are all taking their toll. Conserving and preserving our natural freshwater habitats is increasingly important. It begins with study and understanding. Students of nature are interested in what lives where, and why - and through observation rather than interference. When out on a field trip they have respect for nature, follow the country code, and obey the wildlife laws. If you wish to find out more about ponds and rivers, contact one of the organizations listed on page 64 for guidance on a voyage into nature's watery domain.

THE MICROSCOPIC WORLD
A drop of pond water may look clear, but under a microscope such as this, it will be teeming with tiny water plants and animals. Magnification of about 20X to 200X is most useful.

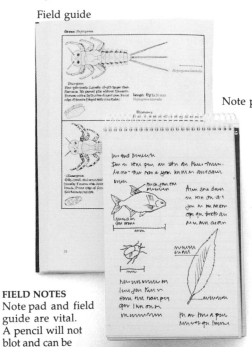

Field guide

Note pad

LOOKING THROUGH LENSES
Magnifiers enable you to identify small water creatures or examine a flower's structure. A 10X lens is about right.

Magnifying glasses

Screw-top glass jars

SHORT-STAY HOMES
Screw-top glass jars are useful for temporary storage and examination. Do not leave animals and plants in them for long.

SPOON AND BRUSH
These pieces of equipment enable small, delicate plants and animals to be moved for study and then replaced without harm.

DISHES AND DROPPERS
These allow small items to be moved gently and studied without too much disturbance.

Plastic spoons

Glass dish

Dropper

FIELD NOTES
Note pad and field guide are vital. A pencil will not blot and can be sharpened carefully with a pocket knife.

FARM WASTE
Accidental spillage of farm wastes into this river killed chub, dace, roach - and thousands of smaller animals.

Waterproof camera

DAMP-PROOF SNAPS
Modern waterproof cameras allow photographs to be taken in the wettest places, even in the spray of a fast stream. Photos record nature without disturbing it.

The dangers of pollution

Ponds, rivers, and other freshwater habitats are under constant threat of pollution. Fertilizers, pesticides, and other farming chemicals are washed through the soil by rain and into watercourses, where they may badly affect the balance of nature. Industrial wastes that may enter rivers can damage water life for long stretches downstream. Most authorities have clean-water laws, but these are not always observed; "accidents" happen, and inspectors cannot monitor every backwater. We can all contribute, by reporting suspicions to the authorities, or by volunteering to help clean out and restock a weed-choked pond, or by clearing a stream used as a rubbish tip.

Folding pocket knife

Plant cutter

Plastic bags and ties

Fine-mesh sieve

WATERPROOFING
Aquatic plants dry out
quickly in air. Keep them
wet by carrying them in
plastic bags.

A CLEAN CUT
Take plant samples only with permission,
and with a sharp blade for minimum damage.

Fork

Trowel

SIEVE FOR SORTING
A fine-mesh sieve can
be rocked gently in
water to sort small
animals from mud
and silt.

TAKING A SAMPLE
A bucket on a string
can be tossed from a
bridge, bank, or boat
to sample the water.

Sealable plastic containers

SPLASH-PROOF CONTAINERS
Pack animals carefully in
sealable containers, using
waterweed as "padding"
to minimize splashing.

SMALL DIGGERS
If you are permitted to dig up plants
or search for muddy-bottom
creatures, use a clean, sharp
fork or trowel and take
great care.

Water-sampling
bucket

Large-mesh net

Fine-mesh net

NET RESULTS
Nets have different mesh
(sizes) for large or small specimens.
Be careful not to uproot plants.
After sorting, replace the net's contents in the water
as quickly as possible.

Index

Useful addresses

American Fisheries Society
5410 Grosvenor Lane,
Suite 100,
Bethesda, MD 20814-2199

National Wetlands
Conservation Project
c/o Nature Conservancy
1800 North Kent Street,
Suite 800,
Arlington, VA 22209

Sierra Club
330 Pennsylvania
Avenue, S.E.
Washington, D.C. 20003

National Audubon Society
National Capital Office,
645 Pennsylvania
Avenue, S.E.
Washington, D.C.
20036-2266

National Wildlife
Federation
1400 16th Street, N.W.
Washington, D.C.
20036-2266

U.S. Fish and
Wildlife Service
Publication Unit,
1717 H Street, N.W.,
Room 148
Washington, D.C. 20240

Acknowledgments

Picture credits
t=top b=bottom m=middle l=left r=right

Heather Angel: 43tr; 45br; 53br
G.I. Bernard/Oxford Scientific Films: 51ml
B.Borrell/Frank Lane Picture Agency: 39m
Bridgeman Art Library: 34tr
British Museum/Natural History: 48tl
B.B.Casals/Frank Lane Picture Agency: 39t
John Clegg: 47tl
G.Dore/Bruce Coleman Ltd: 48mr; 60tr
Fotomas Index: 39ml
C.B. and D.W. Frith/Bruce Coleman Ltd: 41br
Tom and Pam Gardener/Frank Lane Picture Agency: 38br
D.T. Grewcock/Frank Lane Picture Agency: 62br

Mark Hamblin/Frank Lane Picture Agency: 39bm
David Hosking/Eric and David Hosking: 27m; 37ml
Mansell Collection: 13m, tr, ml; 35ml; 49br
L.C. Marigo/Bruce Coleman Ltd: 42bl
Mary Evans Picture Library: 22tl; 23tr; 30bl; 40tr
Dr Morley Reed/Science Photo Library: 39bl
Jany Sauvanet/Natural History Photographic Agency: 40ml
Richard Vaughan/Ardea: 58mr
Roger Wilmshurst/Frank Lane Picture Agency: 29t

Illustrations by Coral Mula: 34bl; 36ml, bl, br; 35tl; ml; 38ml, m; 39mt

Picture research by: Millie Trowbridge

Dorling Kindersley would like to thank:
The Booth Museum of Natural History, Brighton.
Ed Wade, and Respectible Reptiles, Hampton, for help with the amphibians and reptiles.
Richard Harrison and Robert Hughes, Upwey Trout Hatchery, for help with the trout eggs.
Jane Parker for the index.
Fred Ford and Mike Pilley of Radius Graphics, and Ray Owen for artwork.
Anne-Marie Bulat for her work on the initial stages of the book.
Carole Ash, Neville Graham and Martyn Foote for design assistance.
Kim Taylor for special photography on page 27.
Dave King for special photography on pages 2-5, 28-31, 36-7, 52-3 and 62-3.

The author would like to thank:
Don Bentley for loan of equipment;
Mike Birch of Mickfield Fish Centre; Max Bond and Tim Watts of Framlingham Fisheries;
CEL Trout Farm, Woodbridge;
Keith Chell and Chris Riley of Slapton Ley Field Centre; Wendy and David Edwards, Ellen and Chris Nall, Jacqui and Tony Storer for allowing their ponds to be sampled; David "Biggles" Gooderham and Jane Parker for help with collecting; Andrea Hanks and staff at Thornham Magna Field Centre; Alastair MacEwan for technical advice; Ashley Morsely for fish care; Richard Weaving of Dawlish Warren Nature Reserve; John Wortley, Andy Wood and colleagues at Anglian Water Authority.